COPYRIGHT

346·0482 COR

int **3**

for

inf

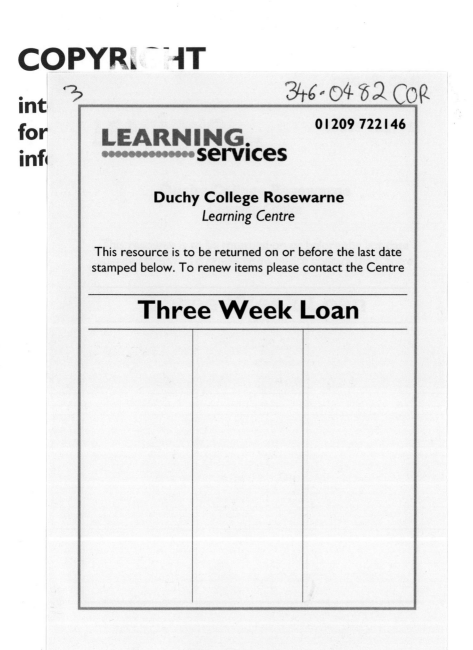

01209 722146

LEARNING.
••••••••••••services

Duchy College Rosewarne
Learning Centre

This resource is to be returned on or before the last date
stamped below. To renew items please contact the Centre

Three Week Loan

Revised Third Edition

COPYRIGHT

interpreting the law for libraries, archives and information services

Graham P. Cornish
Copyright Officer, British Library

LIBRARY ASSOCIATION PUBLISHING
LONDON

Published by
Library Association Publishing
7 Ridgmount Street
London WC1E 7AE

Library Association Publishing is wholly owned by The Library Association.

First published 1990
Second edition 1997
Third edition 1999
This revised third edition 2001

British Library Cataloguing in Publication Data
A catalogue record for this book is available from the British Library.

ISBN 1-85604-409-2

Typeset in Humanist 521 and Garamond by Library Association Publishing.
Printed and made in Great Britain by MPG Books Ltd, Bodmin, Cornwall.

Contents

Author's note

This book tries to set out the basics of UK copyright law, concentrating on those areas which may affect librarians, information professionals and archivists in their daily work. There are many areas which have not been dealt with at length such as public performance, aspects of broadcasting and publishing, and the whole area of design and patents is left to others far more competent to deal with them in those areas where they impinge on the work of libraries and information centres. Neither is it intended as a scholarly textbook but rather as a working tool for the practitioner who is faced with actual situations which need to be resolved in an informed and sensible way. It can be used as a desktop reference work for anyone planning library, archive and information services, or kept at the enquiry desk to help decide what can, or cannot, be done for a reader. The author's hope is that it will be as helpful to junior counter staff as senior managers. It is also aimed at all types of library, archive and information service, whether public, academic, government or private. Attention is given to the different legal situations in which various services function. As would be expected the book focuses on UK law, which it aims to interpret, and the answers found here should never be assumed to apply in other countries. Nevertheless, many of the questions raised are equally valid in any part of the world and should help professionals in other countries to address the issues facing their own libraries.

It is organized on a question and answer pattern to simplify searching for particular problems and their possible solutions. Because of this there is a small amount of repetition between sections. This is quite deliberate to avoid unnecessary 'see also' comments which tend to confuse or bewilder the user. Obviously not every possible question can be answered but every effort has been made to anticipate those which arise most often. The feedback from many users of previous editions of this book has been most useful in amplifying some of the paragraphs in this edition. The law is not there to deal in specific terms with any and every possible situation but to provide the framework within which decisions can be made in specific circumstances. There are always 'grey' areas of interpretation or circumstance when the law will be unclear. Where this is obviously the case, the book tries to offer guidance rather than provide a definite answer as this is just not always possible. Although some of the legislation is still very new, other elements have been in place long enough to make it possible to give some further guidance in areas which were 'fuzzy' when earlier editions were produced. It should be remembered that what the law does not allow can often be done with the copyright owner's consent through an appropriate licence. Therefore, where the book says that the law prevents something, librarians and archivists should first check to see what kind of licence, if any, their institution holds for copying beyond the stated limits. For this reason a chapter on licences has been included in the sure and certain knowledge that it will soon become out of date in such a fast-moving area. In a book of this kind it is not possible to say exactly what existing licences allow as they will differ between different kinds of institution and will change with time but general indications have been given as general guidance.

The author has been advising the British Library on copyright matters for several years and took part in many of the discussions which helped to shape the library profession's reaction to the new legislation and the many Statutory Instruments which have followed the main legislation. He has also been involved in many similar discussions in Brussels and Luxembourg which have implemented many directives which have in their turn caused UK law to be further amended. He served (and serves) on a number of working groups and committees dealing with copyright matters, and has lectured and run seminars on copyright law both in the UK and abroad. He is also involved in a number of initiatives designing and implementing Electronic Copyright Management Systems (ECMS) which will play a major role in the future development of information work world-wide. The wealth of information and opinion gathered from these contacts has been used to compile this book, but it must be remembered it is written by a librarian trying to understand the law, not a lawyer trying to understand libraries!

Assertion of rights

The author asserts his right, as set out in sections 77 and 78 of the Copyright, Designs and Patent Act 1988, to be identified as the author of this work wherever it is published commercially and whenever any adaptation of this work is published or produced, including any sound recordings or films made of, or based upon, this work.

Graham P. Cornish
British Library
Boston Spa

Disclaimer

Whilst the advice and information contained in this book are believed to be true and accurate at the date of going to press, neither the author, the British Library nor The Library Association can accept any legal responsibility or liability for any errors or omissions that may be made.

Acknowledgements

Nobody knows everything about copyright. Consequently, anyone who writes a book on the subject must be indebted to others working in the field. This is certainly true of this author and I would like in particular to thank my friend and sparring partner Sandy Norman, who is Copyright Adviser to The Library Association and for some time fulfilled a similar role for IFLA; Jeremy Phillips, with whom I have taught copyright on various courses for several years; David List for his invaluable help with questions on photographs; and, above all, the many people who have taken part in the numerous copyright workshops throughout the country at which I have taught and whose questions have so enriched this edition.

List of abbreviations

AACR2	Anglo-American Cataloguing Rules Second Edition
ALCS	Authors Licensing and Collecting Society
BLAISE	British Library Automated Information Service
BNB	British National Bibliography
BPI	British Phonographic Industries
BSI	British Standards Institution
CCC	Copyright Clearance Center
CLA	Copyright Licensing Agency
DACS	Design & Artists Copyright Society
DSC	British Library Document Supply Centre
ERA	Educational Recording Agency
HMSO	Her Majesty's Stationery Office
MCPS	Mechanical Copyright Protection Society
NHS	National Health service
NLA	Newspaper Licensing Agency
OCLC	Online Computer Library Center
OCR	optical character recognition
OHP	overhead projector

OS   Ordnance Survey
PLR   Public Lending Right
PRS   Performing Right Society
SDI   Selective Dissemination of Information
SI   Statutory Instruments
USGPO   United States Government Printing Office
VAT   value added tax
WIPO   World Intellectual Property Organisations

Introduction

The idea behind copyright is rooted in certain fundamental ideas about creativity and possession. Basically, it springs from the idea that anything we create is an extension of 'self' and should be protected from general use by anyone else. Coupled with this is the idea that the person creating something has exclusive rights over the thing created, partly for economic reasons but also because of this extension of 'self' idea. Copyright is therefore important to ensure the continued growth of writing, performing and creating. Copyright law aims to protect this growth but, at the same time, tries to ensure that some access to copyright works is allowed as well. Without this access creators would be starved of ideas and information to create more copyright material.

Libraries and information centres are in a unique position as custodians of copyright material. They have the duty to care for, and allow access to, other people's copyright works. This places special responsibilities on all those working in libraries, archives and the information world generally. We practise our profession by using this property so we should take all possible steps to protect it, whilst, at the same time, ensuring that the rights and privileges of our users are also safeguarded.

Because copyright is such an intangible thing, there is often a temptation to ignore it. Those who take this approach forget that they, too, own copyright in their own creations and would feel quite angry if this were abused by others. Some of the restrictions placed on use by the law may seem petty or trivial but they are designed to allow some use of copyright material without unduly harming the interests of the creator (author).

The 1988 Copyright Act, and the many subsequent Statutory Instruments which interpret and modify it, differ substantially from the one of 1956, and anyone familiar with the old Act should not make any assumptions as to the content of the new one. Indeed, anyone who has become familiar with the 1988 Act should not make any assumptions about the current application of it, as it has been modified extensively in the last ten years. Many definitions have changed, new rights have been introduced, lending and rental now play a much more prominent role in the law as it relates to libraries and information centres than previously, and licensing as a concept is firmly established by the Act.

The introduction of new legislation often has the effect of heightening awareness of the subject, making people more keen to know their rights and privileges, and generally creating an atmosphere of extreme caution in case anyone puts a foot wrong and ends up in court. Whilst this is a good thing, nobody should become too paranoid. Although there has been a recent tendency for copyright infringement cases to be heard in criminal courts, this is usually where important commercial considerations apply such as republishing or reproduction in bulk for commercial purposes. Most infringements of copyright by individuals are dealt with through the civil courts so that the rights owner must take legal proceedings if it is thought an infringement has taken place. As there are no cases at present involving libraries as such, it would be reasonable to assume that a similar route would be taken, given that libraries are not, or should not be, involved in mass reproduction for commercial gain!

The Act also set the stage for a completely new approach to the use of copyright material. We all know what the law says (even if we do not always know what it means!) so there is scope to develop services outside the exceptions which the Copyright Act makes by talking to the licensing agencies and other rights owners' organizations to negotiate use of material in return for royalties. Those working in the information industries should not lose sight of this as a real way forward when the law inhibits the introduction of new services without the owners' consent. Licences granted by copyright owners can also override the limitations set by the law.

This third revised edition of *Copyright* takes account of the very latest legislation on databases with a detailed chapter which explains the new law in straightforward terms and answers some of the questions that it is likely to provoke. Opportunity has also been taken to update other areas in the light of more detailed consideration of the legal texts and research undertaken in the area. The implications of the latest case law have also been included. A completely new index has been provided and the list of useful addresses, websites and further reading has also been updated.

Readers should be aware (and beware) that a new Directive on copyright is making its way through the bureaucracy of the European Union at present (January 2001). Eventually it will be implemented in the UK and this is likely to have a major impact on copyright law in this country and throughout the EU. Current wisdom leads us to believe this new legislation may hit the Statute Book in 2003 when a completely new edition of this book will be needed.

Definition and law

1   What is copyright?

Copyright is, in the UK, primarily a property right intended to protect the rights of those who create works of various kinds. The protection is to prevent exploitation of their works by others. It follows that copyright cannot exist by itself but only within the work which has been created. For this reason we say that copyright 'subsists' rather than exists.

2   If it is primarily a property right, what other aspects does it have?

It is also a moral right. This means that the author has certain rights which are not necessarily economic (which is the main point about property rights).

3   What are these moral rights?

Essentially to be named as the author (although this exists in the UK for certain kinds of work only), and not to have works falsely attributed to someone else or to have works falsely attributed to you! There are also rights not to have the work changed in any major way by adding, deleting or changing it. These vary somewhat for artistic works and films. They are dealt with in more detail in Section 3. Note that the author must assert moral rights in writing otherwise there is no infringement of these rights.

4   Are moral rights important for libraries?

Yes, especially in electronic documents (see Section 9).

5   Can copyright subsist even if the original work has disappeared or been destroyed?

Yes. If, for example, a painting was photographed and then destroyed, there would still be copyright in the original painting, even though it did not exist, through the existence of the photograph.

6   What is the latest legislation?

The Copyright, Designs and Patents Act 1988 which came into force on 1 August 1989, subsequent Statutory Instruments and the supporting Regulations. There are a number of these but the Statutory Instruments which affect libraries and archives most are listed below. Items in **bold** are of particular significance to the user of this book.

SI 89/816 Copyright Designs and Patents Act 1988 (Commencement No. 1) Order.

SI 89/1012 Copyright (Recordings of Folksongs for Archives) (Designated Bodies) Order

SI 89/1067 Copyright (Application of Provisions relating to Educational Establishments to Teachers) (No. 2) Order

SI 89/1068 Copyright (Educational Establishments) (No.2) Order.

SI 89/1098 The Copyright (Material Open to Public Inspection) (International Organizations) Order

SI 89/1099 The Copyright (Material Open to Public Inspection) (Making of Copies of Maps) Order

SI 89/1212 Copyright (Librarians and Archivists) (Copying of Copyright Materials) Regulations

SI 99/1751 The Copyright (Application to Other Countries) Order 1999

SI 90/2510 The Copyright (Recording for Archives of Designated Class of Broadcasts and Cable Programmes) (Designated Bodies) (No. 2) Order

SI 92/3233 Copyright (Computer Programs) Regulations 1992.

SI 95/3297 Copyright Rights in Performances: the Duration of Copyright and Rights in Performances Regulations 1995

SI 96/191 Copyright (Certification of Licensing Scheme for Educational Recording of Broadcasts and Cable Programmes) (Educational Recording Agency Limited) (Amendment) Order 1996

SI 99/3452 The Copyright (Certification of Licensing Scheme for Educational Recording of Broadcasts and Cable Programmes) (Educational Recording Agency Limited) (Amendment) Order 1999

SI 96/2967 Copyright and Related Rights Regulations 1996

SI 97/3032 Copyright: Rights in Databases Regulations 1997.

It is important to note that a number of defective Statutory Instruments were drawn up for this Act and never implemented. The above list includes all those of direct relevance to libraries and archives. Other SIs with the same title but different numbering were replaced by those listed and the earlier ones should be ignored. This also applies to some SIs which became out-of-date and were effectively updated with replacements. It should also be noted that a number of terms used in the legislation are not defined. Most of these will be dealt with in the following text but include 'original', 'substantial' (and 'substantially'), 'reasonable' (and 'reasonably'), 'librarian', 'fair dealing' and 'periodical'.

It should also be noted that most (but not quite all) of the 1988 Act does not apply to the Channel Islands which are still subject to either the 1956 Act or even parts of the 1911 Act. The Isle of Man passed its own copyright legislation in 1991 so that the copyright part of this Act (Part 1) no longer applies there. The Manx legislation is sufficiently similar to UK law not to cause major problems.

2

What is covered by copyright?

7   What things are covered by copyright?

Virtually anything that is printed, written, recorded in any form, or anything that can be made by a human being. The law divides these items into various classes and all aspects of them are dealt with separately in the following pages.

8   Does absolutely anything in these groups qualify for copyright?

No, not quite. Works first published in, or by nationals of, certain countries are not protected (see paragraphs 626–7). Also the work has to be original and not trivial, and is not eligible for copyright unless it is recorded in some form. Some items, such as patents, qualify technically for copyright but an international agreement between patent offices has waived all protection of patents for non-commercial copying.

9   What does 'original' mean?

The law does not say, but the idea is that to be protected the author must have contributed quite a lot of their own ideas or skills to the making of the work.

Example. If you write your own poem about Jack and Jill, it is protected. If you simply reproduce the well-known nursery rhyme with one or two minor changes, that is not original and not protected (but the typographical arrangement may be, see paragraph 94ff).

10   What constitutes 'trivial'?

This is not defined but a primitive doodle or a simple 'x' would not qualify, although what is 'simple' and what is not is open to debate!

11   What does 'recorded' mean?

Fixed in some way such as written on paper, stored in a computer system, recorded on a disc (vinyl, CD(-ROM)) or on a film. A live performance which is not recorded or videoed, for example, would not attract copyright.

12   Is the title of a book or journal article protected by copyright?

Rarely. Such titles are statements of fact – they tell you what the book or article is called – and cannot therefore be protected unless they are so complex that they become a literary work in their own right or are registered as a trademark. In this case the problem would arise only if the 'make-up' of the new work looked so like the first work that one could be mistaken for the other.

13   Is there copyright in facts?

No. A fact is a fact and cannot be protected as such. However, the way in which information about facts is presented is protected.

Example. Times of trains are facts and nobody can prevent you from publishing information that trains leave at certain times for particular places provided that you do not take so much information that it damages the rights of the owner (see Section 9 on Databases). What is protected is (a) the layout of the timetable and (b) the actual typography. So you might make this information available by including it in a brochure about a tourist attraction but it would be an infringement to photocopy the timetable and reprint this in the brochure.

14 What about works which are illegal such as pornography?

Just because a work is pornographic, libellous or irreligious, this does not mean it is not protected by copyright. On the other hand, courts have sometimes refused to uphold copyright in such works where a claim for infringement has occurred. The problem is, as always in such matters, what is pornographic today may be entirely acceptable tomorrow. Thus there will be copyright in such works but it may be difficult to enforce.

15 Are things like trademarks and logos protected by copyright?

Yes. A logo is an artistic work and a trademark may well be an artistic work and/or a literary work as well. It is quite possible for a trademark to go out of copyright but still be a trademark as trademarks can last indefinitely. Therefore it could be allowed to copy an old trademark provided it was not used in such a way that it was not also used as a trademark. For example, it might be possible to illustrate a book on advertising with pictures of out-of-copyright trademarks provided they are just pictures and not used to market a product.

16 What are the qualifications necessary to claim copyright?

The person claiming to be the author must be a UK citizen or a citizen of a country where UK works are protected in the same way as in Britain (see paragraphs 626–7). A complete list of these countries is given in SI 99/1751. Also anyone carrying out work for the Crown, Parliament, the United Nations, or the Organization of American States, has that work protected as if it were published in the UK, even if the author is a national of a country not otherwise covered by these arrangements. See also paragraphs 626–7.

17 Are any works excepted from the usual copyright protection?

Yes. The Bible, the Book of Common Prayer of the Church of England and Sir James Barrie's *Peter Pan* all enjoy special protection outside normal copyright limitations. The Authorized Version of the Bible and the Book of Common Prayer are printed under patents issued by the Crown and are therefore in perpetual copyright. This does not extend to modern versions of the Bible, which must be treated as published works which are anonymous, whatever one's personal theological view! The Authorized Version of the Bible and BCP cannot be copied as they are outside copyright law. Permission is usually given for small quotations in published versions, and photocopying of various portions for research or private study or reading in church or chapel is usually allowed. In the case of *Peter Pan*, the Copyright Act brought in perpetual copyright in this play for the benefit of the Hospital for Sick Children, Great Ormond Street, London, provided it remains as a hospital. The Hospital owned the copyright, which expired on 31 December 1987 and obtained a considerable revenue from it. Parliament decided to continue this privilege and any commercial publication or performance of the work attracts a royalty for the Hospital. This is a form of compulsory licensing for a work now out of copyright. As the Act did not come into force until 1 August 1989, any act of copying, commercial publication or performance done between 31 December 1987 and 31 July 1989 was not an infringement. The play cannot be publicly performed without royalty payment to the Hospital for Sick Children. However, as these arrangements are very similar to those for revived copyright (see paragraph 36) it is unclear which regulations will take precedence, should they differ, during the period of revived copyright, which will last until 2007.

18 Is the whole and every little bit of a work protected?

No. Copyright is limited by excluding from protection less than a substantial part of a work. So if less than a substantial part is used or copied there is no infringement except in certain areas.

19 What constitutes a substantial part?

This is not defined. What is clear is that it is not just a question of quantity but of quality as well.

Example. Someone copies a page from a 250-page novel. It is unlikely that this one page is a substantial part of the whole work unless it was the last page of a 'whodunit' which gave away the whole plot. Someone else copies the recommendations and conclusions (three paragraphs) from a 70-page technical report. This is almost certainly a substantial part. Similarly, four bars of a symphony could constitute a substantial part because they encapsulate the theme music of the whole work.

20 So are there any guidelines?

Not really. Each case must be a matter of professional judgment.

Authors' and owners' rights

Authors and owners may, or may not be the same person. They enjoy different rights so this distinction is important. As authors are defined differently for different types of work, they will be dealt with separately in each section. However, despite some variations, their moral rights are similar in all circumstances and can be covered in this section. This section then sets out who the owner is and what the owner is entitled to do exclusively in law. All rights also have limitations in order to exercise them, so the law limits these exclusive rights in a number of ways. This section should therefore be interpreted in the light of what is said later about other people being allowed to do certain acts as well. It is these exceptions which form the bulk of this book.

Moral rights

21   What are moral rights?

Moral rights are designed to protect the idea that anything created contains an element of 'self' in it. Therefore the author ought to be able to protect certain aspects of a work. The law is complex in this area and most library services will not have major concerns with moral rights so no attempt is made to give an exhaustive description of them.

22   What rights does the author acquire under this law?

For authors of literary works the rights are:

- to have the author's name included when the work is published
- to prevent significant parts of the work being removed
- to prevent significant additions being made to the work
- to prevent significant alterations to the work
- to prevent someone else's name being added to the work
- to prevent works being attributed to someone when they did not create them.

These rights vary slightly depending on whether or not the work is intended to be sung or spoken to music.

For authors of artistic works, 'published' is extended to exhibiting, broadcasting or including the work in a film.

23   Do these rights apply in all cases?

No. For literary works, essentially they apply only to monographs. They also apply to films and artistic works of all kinds. They do not apply where the work was carried out as part of the author's employment.

Ownership of copyright

24   Ownership of copyright is a complex question

Copyright is a property and can be disposed of in the same way as other property so ownership is not always easy to identify. The author may have assigned the copyright to someone else. It may have been sold to a publisher, given to someone else, left to someone in a will or automatically transferred to an employer, the Crown or Parliament. In 1996 the law changed, extending copyright protection in many cases from 50 to 70 years after death. This gave rise to 'extended' copyright (where 20 years has been added on to existing copyright) and 'revived' copyright (where a work was out of copyright because the author had been dead for more than 50 years but because they had been dead less than 70 years copyright came back into force).

25   Is the copyright in a work one single piece of property or can it be broken up?

Copyright is a quite complicated bundle of rights (see paragraph 49ff) and these can be sold or leased to different people. They can also be sold for a limited period so that one person may have one bundle of rights for 10 years then buy them for a further 30 years and so on. This is particularly important for works made into films or plays, musicals, operas and ballets.

26   Someone must start the ownership process. Who owns copyright first?

Copyright is usually owned first of all by the author.

27   Why 'usually'?

Because there are different rules depending on employment or commissioning.

28   How does employment come into ownership?

If authors create a work as part of their job, then their employer is usually the owner. However, there can be a contract between employer and employee which can state the opposite is required (i.e. the copyright remains with the employee). See the notes on commissioned works in paragraph 29. There are special arrangements for Crown and Parliamentary Copyright (see paragraphs 37–8). Also the author is differently defined for different classes of work such as films and sound recordings. Most of the legislation is actually about the rights enjoyed by the owner of copyright rather than the author. For this reason most authors' economic rights are referred to as 'owner's rights'.

29 Supposing the work was commissioned?

If the work was commissioned after 1 August 1989, the copyright is owned by the author. Before that date it is usually the property of the person who paid for the commission.

30 Supposing a library owns an original work such as a manuscript. Does the library own the copyright?

No. It is important to distinguish between the object and the copyright which subsists in it. The library may own the manuscript but the copyright is still owned by the author or the person by whom it has been sold or assigned, so the library has no right to reproduce the manuscript, except as allowed by the exceptions in the Copyright Act. However, the library may enjoy other rights over the manuscript under Publication Right (see paragraph 326ff). When a library or archive has unpublished material bequeathed to it through the will of the original author, it is assumed that the copyright also becomes the property of the library or archive unless the owner stipulated otherwise.

31 Who owns the copyright in a letter?

The author, that is, the person who wrote the letter.

32 Why does the person who received the letter not own it?

Because copyright belongs to the person who creates the work. The letter itself does belong to the person who received it. They were given it by the writer. But the copyright still belongs to the writer not the recipient of the letter.

33 What about a letter sent to the editor of a newspaper or journal?

Technically the copyright still belongs to the writer of the letter although, by sending the letter to the editor in the first place, there is an assumption that the writer wished it to be published and therefore the editor has an *implied* licence to publish. This does not give the editor or the publisher any other rights over the use of the letter.

34 Who owns the copyright in a periodical issue?

Each author of an article in a periodical issue owns the copyright in that article but the publisher owns the copyright in the issue as a whole including the typographical arrangement (see paragraph 94ff).

Example. Someone writes an article for a periodical. Unless they sign an agreement to the contrary, they retain the copyright in the article and have the right to have it published elsewhere. But they do not have the right simply to photocopy the article as first published and have it republished in that form. This would infringe the typographical copyright of the publisher. For the same reason the author cannot simply make multiple photocopies of the article for friends and colleagues.

35 Who owns 'extended copyright'?

Essentially the person who owned the copyright immediately before the extended copyright came into force. See paragraph 24.

36 Who owns 'revived copyright'?

The person who owned the copyright immediately before it expired. If that person is dead, or the body owning the copyright has ceased to exist then the copyright is owned by the personal representatives of the author. See paragraph 24.

37 Who owns Crown Copyright?

Technically, the Crown. However, Crown Copyright is administered by HMSO which, although now privatized, still has a residual responsibility to administer copyright owned by the Crown.

38   Who owns the copyright in a Parliamentary Bill or Act of Parliament?

The copyright in a Bill belongs to whichever House introduced the Bill first. When the Bill becomes an Act it becomes Crown copyright.

39   Supposing a work is out of print. Does the publisher still own the copyright?

This will depend on the contract between the author and the publisher but, generally speaking, copyright in a work reverts to the author if the work goes out of print and the publisher has no plans to reprint or republish the work. However, the publisher will retain the copyright in the typography of the work (see paragraph 94ff).

40   What rights does the law give the copyright owner?

Copyright law gives the owner exclusive rights to do certain things to or with the copyright material. Nobody else is entitled to do these things. There are six basic rights:

- to copy the work
- to issue copies to the public
- to perform, show or play the work
- to broadcast the work
- to adapt the work
- to rent or lend the work.

Each of these rights will be examined under the appropriate type of work. Those who own rights in databases or performances have quite different rights.

41   Are these absolute rights or do other people have some rights to use the material as well?

They are not absolute because they are limited by (a) time, (b) quantity/quality, (c) purpose and (d) certain exemptions given to user groups. Each of these limitations will be examined under the appropriate type of work. But it is important to note that the limitations set for use of copyright material are exceptions to the rights of owners and not rights enjoyed by users.

42   Do these rights last for ever?

No. They are limited by various periods of time, which vary according to the type of material and the circumstances in which it is kept. See individual sections for the duration of copyright in different types of material.

Literary, dramatic and musical works

These three classes are dealt with together because they are all treated in a similar way under the Copyright Act, although there are some differences for some specific areas. In addition, a printed text also has a copyright in the typographical arrangement of the work concerned, regardless of the copyright status of the content of the text. Any literary work which will also qualify as a database is subject to special rules. See Section 9 for details

Definitions

Literary works

43   What is a literary work?

The term 'literary work' includes anything that is printed or written such as books, journals, technical reports and manuscripts, and also covers any works that are spoken or sung. It also includes compilations (statistical, timetables, but those are more likely to be databases (see Section 9)) as well as computer programs and text stored electronically.

Examples. The words of a popular song are protected as a literary work; the music is treated separately (see paragraph 50ff). The handwritten notes of an author are protected just as much as the final printed book. Railway timetables are protected as compilations although individual pieces of information within the timetable are not.

44   Does 'literary' mean it has to be good quality literature?

No. Copyright law says almost nothing about the quality or content of the work, although case law shows that trivial works are not eligible for protection. Literary means anything which is written, spoken or sung which has been recorded, whether in writing or some other way.

45   What about databases? Are these covered by copyright?

Yes, they certainly are! A database is now largely a separate type of work. See Section 9.

46   Are bibliographic records covered by copyright?

This is a difficult question and has never been clarified in law. The question is: is a bibliographic record 'original'? Originality requires some intellectual input from the author. Most bibliographic records consist of a series of facts presented in a predetermined order according to AACR2 or other cataloguing codes of practice. In theory, everyone using these codes should produce exactly the same record. The fact that they do not is more to do with human fallibility than the rules themselves! But it could be argued that human intellect had been used to implement the rules. Therefore it would be difficult to decide whether a catalogue record has any copyright as such, although the typography in a published catalogue would be protected (see paragraph 94ff).

47   So are bibliographies not protected by copyright?

Almost any bibliography will now qualify as a database rather than a literary work and must be treated accordingly. The one exception is the scholarly bibliography, which may be annotated and is prepared by one identifiable person. See Section 9 and paragraph 62 for detailed information.

48   Is a library catalogue protected?

A library catalogue is almost certainly a database and will be protected as such under copyright law. See Section 9.

Dramatic works

49   What is the difference between a literary and a dramatic work?

A dramatic work is the non-spoken part of a presentation and includes dance and mime. The words of a dramatic work are protected as a literary work.

Example. A show like *West Side Story*, will have separate copyrights in the words (literary work), the choreography and directions (dramatic work) and the music (musical work).

Musical works

50   Does 'musical work' mean anything with music included?

No. Musical work means only the music and excludes the words (which are a literary work) and any actions which go with the music (because they are dramatic works).

Example. West Side Story (as mentioned above in 'dramatic works') will have three separate copyrights: (1) in the words; (2) in the actions and movements of the singers; (3) in the musical notes. Although this may sound complicated it is important, because the people who composed the three elements will each own a separate copyright, which may expire at different times. So the music might go out of copyright but not the words, or vice versa.

51 Does 'musical work' include a recording of the music?

No. That is separately covered as a sound recording (see the section on sound recordings).

52 What about a play performed and recorded on video?

The play is protected as a literary work and the video made of the performance is protected as a film, quite separately. The performers will also have rights in their performances.

Definition of author

It is important to define who the author of a work is as this will usually determine how long copyright lasts. Copyright is most often linked to the death of the author. It is also important to note that the author is defined differently for different types of material but for literary, dramatic, musical and artistic works the definitions are more or less the same.

53 What is the definition of the author?

This varies according to the type of work being considered but for literary, dramatic and musical works it is the person who created the work.

54 Supposing there are two or more authors?

They all count as the authors of the copyright.

55 Supposing it is not possible to find out who the author is?

A work is considered anonymous if the identity of the author cannot be traced by making reasonable inquiries.

56   What does 'reasonable inquiry' mean?

This is not defined but it would presumably require checking in major catalogues and relevant literary dictionaries, etc.

57   Supposing the author's identity is established later on?

Once the author's identity is established, then the work is no longer anonymous and the usual procedures apply.

58   Supposing the author has used a pseudonym?

Unless you can find out whose pseudonym it is, then the work is counted as anonymous. As with anonymous works, this would require reasonable inquiry, i.e. checking of literary reference works and major library catalogues.

59   What happens if a work definitely has more than one author, but not all their names are known?

Once the name of even one author is known, the work is no longer anonymous.

Example. Title page gives: 'Love Poems by the author of "Love Songs" et al'. Once the authorship of 'Love Songs' has been established, the work is not anonymous, even though the identity of 'et al.' may never be known.

60   Supposing the author is given as an organization?

If no person is named as the author the work is treated as anonymous.

61   If a work was generated by a computer, who counts as the author then?

The person who made the necessary arrangements for creating the work (but see Section 9).

62   What about compilations such as directories, timetables, bibliographies and encyclopedias?

If the work has a personal author then that is the author. So a bibliography compiled by someone is protected just as if it were a book. However, something like the *British National Bibliography* has no personal author so is protected only as an anonymous work. Most works like this will qualify as databases (see Section 9) for which separate rules apply.

63   What about works which have lots of articles by different people, such as an encyclopedia which has articles signed by separate people?

Then each article is protected as a separate work, and it may also be a database.

64   Supposing some articles are signed and some not?

They are all treated separately as individual works, so copyright in some will be treated as the work of an author and some will be anonymous.

65   Do moral rights apply to this group of works?

Yes, but only for monographs and not then if the work was prepared as part of the author's employment.

66   What about journal articles and contributions to directories?

These authors do not enjoy moral rights.

Duration of copyright in literary, dramatic and musical works

67   Does copyright last for the same period for all literary, dramatic and musical works?

No. There are different periods of copyright as described below.

Published works

68   What constitutes 'published'?

Published means issuing copies to the public. This in turn means putting into circulation copies not previously put into circulation. Note that the emphasis is on copies. Making a single copy does not of itself constitute publication. The definition also includes making the work available through an electronic retrieval system.

69   How long does copyright last for published literary, dramatic and musical works?

This depends on the country of origin of the work. If the work was published in an EEA country (see paragraph 70) or the author is an EEA national, then the copyright in published literary, dramatic or musical works lasts for 70 years from the end of the calendar year in which the author dies. Copyright always expires on 31 December, never in the middle of a year.

Example. Author died on 5 January 1902; copyright expires on 31 December 1972. Author died on 29 December 1902; copyright still expires on 31 December 1972.

70   What is the EEA?

The European Economic Area, which comprises (as at April 2001): Austria, Belgium, Denmark, Finland, France, Germany, Greece, Iceland, Ireland, Italy, Liechtenstein, Luxembourg, Netherlands, Norway, Portugal, Spain, Sweden, UK.

71   What about works published outside the EEA?

These are protected for the same length of time as they would be in their own country if none of the authors are EEA nationals. If a work is published in a country which gives only 50 years' protection then that is all it will get within the EEA.

72   Supposing it was published simultaneously in several countries both within and outside the EEA?

In this case, it is considered as an EEA publication. Note that 'simultaneous' means within 30 days of first publication. So a work could be published in, say, Australia one day but, provided it was also published in an EEA country within 30 days of that first publication, it would still qualify for EEA protection.

73 Supposing the work is anonymous or has no personal author?

Anonymous works first published within the EEA, which includes works which have no personal author, such as annual reports of organizations or anything with no identifiable personal author, remain in copyright for 70 years from the end of the year in which they are published. Otherwise the work is protected for the length of time it would have been published in the country of origin (usually 50 years).

74 Supposing the author died before the work was published, does this make a difference?

If the work was published after the author died but before 1 January 1969, then copyright expires 50 years from the end of the year in which the work was published. If the author died on or after 1 January 1969 then the 70-year rule applies as in other cases (but see paragraph 71 for non-EEA authors).

Compilations and periodicals

75 What about works made up of contributions by several people?

The copyright expires separately for each contribution. So the copyright in papers in conference proceedings all expire at different times, depending on when each contributor dies. However, the copyright in the typography will expire 25 years after the end of publication (see paragraph 94ff on typographical arrangement).

76   When does the copyright in a periodical issue run out?

The copyright in each article will run out 70 years after the death of the author (as for any other published literary work) but the copyright in the periodical issue as a whole (i.e. the typography) will expire 25 years after publication. If the periodical was published outside the EEA and none of the authors are EEA nationals, then copyright lasts for only as long as the country of publication provides.

77   Supposing the work contains illustrations by someone other than the author?

The copyright in the text and in the illustrations are quite separate. For example, the copyright in the drawings accompanying A. A. Milne's Pooh Bear stories will last much longer than the stories themselves.

Unpublished works

78   What if the work is unpublished?

The situation may sound complicated. If the author died before 1 January 1969, was a national of an EEA state and the work was unpublished at that time, copyright expires on 31 December 2039. If the author died on or after 1 January 1969, the work is protected for 70 years from the end of the year in which the author died. If the author is not a national of an EEA state then copyright expires at the end of the term of protection the author's national laws gives.

Example. Author died 22 November 1955; copyright expires 31 December 2039. Author died 3 December 1990; copyright expires 31 December 2060 (death + 70 years).

79   What if the author is still alive?

Copyright will last until 70 years after the end of the year in which the author dies, just like a published work, or if from outside the EEA, the length of time the author's own nation gives.

80   Does this mean that all unpublished works cannot be used by anyone until 2039?

No. If the work was held by the library or archive before 1 August 1989 and the author was already dead, then these documents can be copied, even with a view to publication, provided that the author has been dead for **50** years if the document is 100 years old.

Example. Author wrote a poem in 1875 and died in 1910. The poem could be copied after 31 December 1975. Note, however, that 'view to publication' does not mean they can be published – only copied in preparation for plans to seek permission to publish.

81   What about anonymous/pseudonymous works?

Unpublished anonymous or pseudonymous works are protected for 70 years from the end of the year in which they are created, or 70 years from being first made available to the public. However, where a work was created before 1 August 1989, copyright protection must last until 2039 regardless of the assumed date of creation. Despite this, if it is reasonable to assume the author has been dead for 50 years then the work can be treated as out of copyright.

82   What happens once anonymous/pseudonymous works are published?

They are protected for 70 years from the end of the year in which they are published. This includes not only publishing but public performance or broadcasting.

83   Supposing it is not possible to judge when a document was created?

There are special provisions for this situation. Where it is not possible by reasonable inquiry to find the identity of the author and it is reasonable to suppose the copyright has expired, then the work may be treated as out of copyright.

84   What constitutes 'reasonable'?

This is not defined. Common sense and professional judgment are needed to make a guesstimate as to when a work might have been written. One learned judge said that 'what is reasonable is what seems reasonable to the man on the Clapham omnibus'.

85   How is the length of copyright worked out if there are several authors?

Where a work has joint authorship, copyright lasts until 70 years after the end of the year in which the last one dies. If at least one of the authors is known, then any unknown ones are disregarded. Where some authors are EEA nationals and others are not, the work is treated as qualifying for the EEA term of protection (death + 70 years) or for 50 years from the death of the last author to die if this gives a longer term of protection.

Example. A work has three authors – two are EEA nationals and one is not. The two EEA nationals die in 1955 and 1960 respectively, giving a term of protection until 2030 but the third, non-EEA author, whose country gives 50 years protection, does not die until 1995, giving protection until 2045.

Crown and Parliamentary copyright

86   What is Crown Copyright?

When a work is created by an employee of the Crown it becomes subject to Crown copyright which is technically owned by the Crown (Her Majesty) and different rules apply to this type of material.

87   Who counts as a Crown employee?

Since the distancing of much civil service work from central government and recent moves to devolution this is no longer clear. Major government departments and ministries are Crown but the status of many bodies (for example the British Library) is unclear.

88   How long does Crown Copyright last?

Crown Copyright lasts for 125 years from the year in which the work was created or 50 years from the year in which it was first commercially published, provided this happens within 75 years of the year of creation. In other words 125 years is the maximum. *Example.* A report is prepared in 1930. Its copyright will run out in 2055. But if it is published commercially, say, in 1960, then the copyright runs out in 2010.

89   What if the author in the example did not die until 1970?

It makes no difference. Length of Crown Copyright is linked to date of creation or date of publication, not the human being responsible for creating the work.

90   Supposing some papers were not released because of the '30 year rule' and were secret until then?

This makes no difference. Copyright runs from the year in which the work was created.

91   What is Parliamentary copyright?

Parliamentary copyright exists in any work commissioned by either or both Houses of Parliament.

92   How long does it last?

It lasts for 50 years from the year in which the work was created.

93   Are the publications of other governments protected in the same way?

No. Publications of other governments are protected as if they were ordinary commercial publications in the UK. In the case of the USA, the US Government claims no copyright in its own publications within the USA and it would seem unlikely that they should be protected in the UK in a way that they are not in the USA. So it is generally assumed that USGPO (United States

Government Printing Office) publications are not protected by copyright.

Typographical arrangements of published editions

94 What is typographical copyright?

Every published work has two copyrights: one in the actual content of the text and the other in the printed layout of the page.

95 Who counts as the author of the typographical arrangement of a work?

The publisher.

96 How long does typographical copyright last?

Typographical copyright lasts for 25 years from the end of the year in which the work is published.

97 So when does the copyright on a published work actually expire?

There are two dates. One, usually the earlier, will be the typographical one which runs out 25 years after first publication. However, the author's copyright continues until 70 (or 50) years after death. So the copyright in a book runs out in two stages. This does nothing to help people who want to copy it within that 25 year period, of course. However, it does allow republication by another publisher if the author has retained the copyright and not assigned it exclusively to the first publisher.

98 Does this mean that every time a book is reprinted the copyright begins again?

No. If the reprint is simply a reproduction of the original typographical arrangement, no new copyright comes into force.

99 Supposing it is a new layout of the book?

Then typographical copyright subsists in that particular edition.

100 What if it is the same typesetting but a long new introduction has been written?

There will be a new copyright in the new introduction, owned originally by the author of that introduction. The publisher can claim copyright in the whole work (introduction and text) together but the original text will only be a reproduction of an earlier text and is covered only for the time that typographical copyright lasts.

Example. Shakespeare is long out of copyright but a new edition of his works will go into copyright for 25 years to protect the typography. This does not stop someone else bringing out their own edition or photocopying older editions that are out of copyright.

101 Do moral rights last for the same length of time?

Yes, but with one important exception. The right not to have works falsely attributed to oneself lasts for only 20 years from the end of the year in which the person dies.

Owners' rights in literary, dramatic, and musical works

Essentially copyright is a monopoly against which certain exceptions are set to make a balance between owner and user. This section begins by looking at the rights that owners of copyright enjoy and then examining how they are limited by exceptions.

Copying

102 Does the owner alone have the right to make copies?

Yes, subject to the limitations mentioned later on.

103 Does copying just mean photocopying?

Certainly not. It means copying in any material form. This includes any method of copying, including, of course, resetting the type to make a new edition for publication, copying by hand or taking a photograph. Photocopying is clearly copying something and there are special provisions to allow some types of copying for some purposes. It also includes electronic copying and this covers storing a work in any form. It also includes copying the text onto a computer disk, converting it to electronically readable text by using Optical Character Recognition (OCR) equipment, storing it on CD-ROM or transmitting it by telefacsimile. This also includes making copies of computer programs for any purpose.

104 Telefacsimile (fax) involves copying. Is the use of fax really an infringement?

Technically, yes. The law says that it is an infringement to store a work in electronic form and making copies which are 'transient or incidental to some other use of the work' are an infringement. These are the two things that are done when a fax message is sent. Having said what the law states, it is sometimes the case that common practice is allowed to continue even though technically illegal. Only time will tell what the position of copyright owners on this issue will be.

105 Documents received by fax often fade and disappear. Can the document be further copied as soon as it is received to make a durable copy?

Not legally. This is just a further copy in the fax chain, all of which seem to be infringing copies.

106 What about microforms?

Making a microform is copying and is not permitted without the owner's consent.

107 What about copying for people with reading handicaps?

There are no provisions for copying for people with reading handicaps in the Act except for subtitling broadcasts or cable programmes for the hard of hearing or persons with other types of handicap. Transcribing works into Braille, making sound recordings of books, enlargements for the visually handicapped or the various copies made by print-to-voice machines are all technically infringements. The law permits licensing schemes for such activities and many copyright owners willingly give their permission, but it should be remembered that this willingness can be eroded if the courtesy of asking first is not observed. See also the discussion of the Copyright Licensing Agency licence, which now allows the making of large print copies in some circumstances. See also the Publishers Licensing Society website for guidelines (**www.pls.org.uk**).

108 How much of a bibliography can be copied?

Only small amounts. See Section 9 for details.

109 Could catalogue records be photocopied and put into a library catalogue?

No. Although each entry might well not attract copyright, there will certainly be copyright in the typography and by cutting up the photocopy and using the entries as catalogue cards this will infringe the typographical arrangement as the use would not be for fair dealing. There will also be a separate Database Right. (The term 'fair dealing' is crucial to understanding much of this book – see paragraph 115ff for more detailed information.)

110 Can copies be made for committee meetings?

No. Copying for committees is multiple copying and is not permitted unless the amount copied is less than substantial. However, in many organizations committee copying would be covered by an appropriate licence.

111 Can a slide (or OHP) be made of a page of a book for teaching in a class or giving a lecture?

Not under the law. The British Copyright Council has said that copying for a 'one-off' lecture to, say, a local history group or for general classroom use would not be regarded by them as an infringement. Alternatively, if less than a substantial part were copied then it would be in order to make a slide of that part.

112   Some books and journals carry a warning that no part of the work can be reproduced, stored, etc. Does this take away the allowances given under the Copyright Act?

This statement has never been tested in law. It is generally thought unlikely that it would stand up in court as it tries to prohibit what the law allows. There is an argument that it constitutes a contract between the publisher and the user about which the user knew perfectly well before buying the book but general opinion is that it is there to frighten rather than be enforced! Actual enforcement of it would be a very difficult thing to do and costly in legal fees to establish as binding. Of course, if it were binding, libraries could refuse to buy the books, which would make a considerable difference to publishers' sales. More recent books by properly informed publishers preface this prohibitive statement with the phrase 'except as permitted by the 1988 Copyright Designs and Patents Act . . .'.

113   Can any copying at all be carried out without permission?

The law makes certain exceptions to the exclusive rights which owners enjoy over their works. The most important for libraries, archives and information providers are certain rights to copy and lend copyright works.

114   For what purposes can a copyright work be copied without the owner's consent?

There are three reasons listed. The most commonly claimed and most frequently quoted is fair dealing.

Fair dealing

115 What is fair dealing?

Fair dealing is a concept which has never been defined. What it seems to be saying is that there may be good reasons for copying something so long as the copying does not harm the copyright owner but nevertheless benefits either the individual or society generally.

116 Does fair dealing apply to all copyright works?

Yes, but the different types of fair dealing apply differently to different classes of material. It applies to literary, dramatic, musical or artistic works for research and private study but not to audiovisual materials such as broadcasts, film, video or sound recordings, although these materials are covered by fair dealing for news reporting, and criticism and review.

117 How much of a work can be copied under fair dealing?

Nobody knows for certain – it is a matter of individual judgment in each case. What is clear is that until a substantial part of a work is copied, there can be no infringement, so such defences as fair dealing are not needed. But see Section 9 when a work is also a database.

118 What is a substantial part?

See paragraph 18ff.

119 So is there no guidance at all?

In the law, no. Various guidelines have been issued in the past but they are guidelines only. The British Copyright Council has issued a set of guidelines, outlining what they think is fair from an owner's viewpoint. Other organizations such as the Ordnance Survey, British Standards Institution and Goad Publishing issue guidelines too, but see Section 10 on licences.

120 What are the justifications for fair dealing?

The law recognizes several. The one most commonly cited in libraries is copying for research or private study. The other purposes are criticism and review and reporting current events.

Research and private study

121 How can anyone judge if copying something is 'fair'?

Look at the amount to be copied in conjunction with the reason for making the copy. No concrete examples can be given but consider the following situations. A student wishes to photocopy a five-verse poem from a collection to study at home; a researcher wishes to publish four out of its five verses in a commercially published criticism of the poet. One is research and private study, the other criticism, both of which are justifications for claiming fair dealing. But the first would seem more likely to be 'fair' than the second. Copying a whole work which has long been out of print and unavailable might be 'fair' but copying the same work just to save buying a copy is obviously not.

122 Can any kind of research qualify?

Yes. The order of words is important – research or private study, not private study or research. Any sort of research can be the reason for claiming fair dealing, including commercial and industrial research. This may change following legislation which has just been passed by the European Parliament.

123 Why private study?

Private study is thought of as being done alone. Therefore multiple copying for classroom use cannot be private study and is provided for separately under educational copying (see below).

124 Is private study limited to students?

Not at all, if by 'student' it is meant someone in an academic institution. Anyone undertaking training or education of any kind, including leisure courses such as evening classes in hobbies or holiday languages, can reasonably claim fair dealing as a 'student'. But to do this the copying must be done by the STUDENT personally and not on behalf of the student.

125   Does fair dealing allow the making of more than one copy?

If the student or researcher does the copying themselves it might be possible to make more than one copy.

Example. Suppose a student has to go on a geography field trip. Two copies of a small portion of a map may be needed – one for use in the field (where it may get muddy or torn) and the other for the file relating to the project. If two copies are made they must be for the personal use only of the person who made them.

126   Supposing the student wants a copy for personal use and one for a friend?

Not allowed! If any copying is done on behalf of someone else then the person making the copy must not make it if they know that this will result in a copy of substantially the same material being supplied to more than one person at substantially the same time and for substantially the same purpose. But always remember that your institution may have a licence which would allow this.

Example. Three students may make for themselves one copy each of, say, a journal article, for use in a lecture or project. But if one makes copies for personal use and copies for the two friends then this is an infringement.

127   What do all these 'substantiallys' mean?

They are not defined but it would seem likely that someone copying pages 9–14 for themselves and 10–16 for a friend or colleague would have copied 'substantially the same material' and that this copying, if done on Monday and Wednesday of the same week for use in the same tutorial or related experiments at the laboratory bench, would constitute at substantially the same time and for substantially the same purpose.

128   What about coin-operated machines then?

Although these are not dealt with specifically, the Act differentiates between copies made by students/researchers themselves and those made for them by other people. Although nothing is said in this context about providing equipment which might be used for infringing purposes it is clear from another part of the Act that it is not an offence to possess equipment which can be used for breach of copyright, as opposed to equipment which can be used only for breach of copyright. It would be foolish of any librarian deliberately to turn a blind eye to copying which was beyond the law and a suitable notice giving details of what is and is not allowed should be displayed (contact The Library Association for a suggested text) but whether a librarian could actually be held responsible is open to doubt. Any notice should refer to the new Copyright Act and its restrictions. These should also be mentioned in any publicity for the library's services and any user education courses which are offered. Generally librarians are expected to use their best endeavours to ensure that machines in their care are not used for infringements of copyright.

129   What if the person asks the librarian to do the copying for them?

What the law says, in a rather roundabout way, is that copying by libraries is only fair dealing if the special conditions about copying by libraries are observed. If the library steps outside these conditions then the copying is not fair dealing and becomes an infringement. Copying by libraries is dealt with in detail in paragraph 152ff.

130   What about downloading from databases?

See the section on databases for detailed guidance.

131   What about databases stored on CD-ROM?

Again, see the section on databases.

132   What about copying from collections of data such as telephone directories?

Such items as telephone directories and timetables are now classed as databases. See Section 9.

133   What about things like *Yellow Pages*?

In the specific case of *Yellow Pages* BT have said that they consider one page or one classified section, whichever is the smaller, to be a reasonable amount to copy. (See also paragraph 18ff).

Criticism or review

134   What other justifications for fair dealing are there?

An important one for librarians of all kinds is criticism or review. It is allowed to quote parts of a work when writing critical essays or reviews such as book reviews in the *Library Association Record* or comparisons of different authors' works in academic research.

135   How much can be quoted?

Again, it is not stated but the publishers used to say that they felt a single extract of up to 400 words or a series of extracts (none of which was over 300 words) totalling not more than 800 words was not unfair. For poems this was given as 40 lines or not more than 25% of the whole poem. These figures are simply to indicate some thinking on the quantities that might be involved. The source of the quotations must be given, e.g. the full bibliographic reference in a review is essential as the reviewer may be encouraging the reader to buy a copy! The same is true if a criticism is being written of the writings of a single author. Libraries which prepare their own reviews for the general public, or in the form of information bulletins for researchers, should note the conditions under which, and to what extent, they can quote the works mentioned.

136 Does this review idea extend to news bulletins?

No. Reporting current events is a separate justification for claiming fair dealing. The production of news bulletins, current events information and similar news items can utilize any news material provided that sufficient acknowledgement of the source is made. Such activities as news clippings services, circulated to staff, are justified on these grounds but each clipping must have the source noted on it. Fair dealing in this context does not extend to photographs. (See also paragraph 561ff.)

Reporting current events

137 What is a current event?

A current event is something defined less by time than by current interest. It can be something which happened yesterday or today, but, equally, it might be something that happened several years ago but which has a bearing on events happening now.

138 Supposing the news items that are needed include a photograph?

Clearly the law is intended to protect the very considerable investment in photography made by newspapers and without this exception any evening paper could use the photographs of any morning one for its news story. In theory this applies to internal and local news bulletins made from clippings but it is very difficult to exclude a photograph in the middle of a piece of news text. Technically it should be blacked out but this is often done in the photocopying process anyway! The alternative is to retype the necessary text. But note that licences are now available for copying some newspapers through the Newspaper Licensing Agency (NLA). Note that the NLA has a limited repertoire as far as literary works are concerned but a wider one for typographical arrangement. This may limit its ability to license some materials. This does not stop you reformatting the actual contents in some way for re-use. However, the whole question of copying newspapers is at present the subject of legal proceedings, the outcome of which may have a major impact on the ability to copy for reporting current events. See Section 10 on Licences.

139   Supposing the news bulletin is prepared and displayed electronically?

The same rules apply as for a clippings service.

Educational copying

See also Section 10 on Licences.

140   Are the amounts allowed to be copied for educational copying just as vague as in fair dealing?

No, the rules are quite different.

141   What is the difference between copying for educational purposes and copying for private study?

Private study does not mean for classroom use. Educational copying can be for classroom use. All librarians in any organization where teaching takes place should be aware of what is allowed as the materials in their care are frequently utilized for educational purposes. This is also true for public libraries which are used for project work. Educational copying exceptions do not apply to training in commercial/industrial companies.

142   Can a teacher or pupil copy anything for use in the classroom?

A teacher or pupil may copy out all or part of a copyright work in the course of instruction (e.g. a poem) onto the blackboard or into an exercise book for the purposes of instruction but they may not copy it using a reprographic process, i.e. not by photo-copying it.

143   Does instruction apply only to schools and universities?

No. Instruction can take place in industrial or commercial training courses, military camps or anywhere else. Note that 'instruction' is not the same thing as 'education' for copyright purposes.

144   What about copying for examinations?

Anything can be copied for the purposes of setting the questions or providing the answers except musical works, which may not be photocopied to allow the pupil to perform the work. A further problem is determining when continuously assessed work counts as part of an examination and when it is classroom teaching.

145   Does 'anything' really mean anything?

Yes, except for musical scores as mentioned above.

146   What if a student needs to include some copyright material in a thesis for a degree?

This would seem to be covered in providing the answers to an examination. There could be problems if the thesis is subsequently copied for other purposes, or published.

147   What happens if several children come into the public library, all asking for copies of the same thing for their project?

Only one copy can be provided. It is unclear at what age a child could sign the necessary declaration form (see paragraph 183ff) as a legal minor. However, schools operated by local authorities usually have a licence to copy necessary materials and the teacher should investigate if this will allow the required materials to be copied.

148   What about including some copyright material in collections put together by teachers?

There are special rules governing this, which should be known by the teacher or publisher and not worry the librarian too much. Section 33 of the Act sets out the limits for this sort of publishing, for which librarians are sometimes asked to provide the original material to copy.

Copying for educational establishments

149 What counts as an educational establishment?

An educational establishment is defined as

- any school
- any university allowed to award degrees under Act of Parliament or Royal Charter
- any institution empowered to offer further or higher education under the Education (Scotland) Act 1980, the Education and Libraries (Northern Ireland) Order 1986 or the Education Reform Act 1988 (see SI 98/1068 for exact details)
- any theological college.

150 Multiple copying is not allowed and fair dealing does not extend to classroom copying, so what can be done for teachers who need multiple copies of parts of works for use in instruction? Surely they do not have to rely on writing everything out by hand?

No! The Act allows one of two ways forward. If a licence is obtainable to cover the needed materials, then that licence should be taken out and adhered to. All local authorities and many universities have taken out such a licence and the first thing is to check what it covers and what it allows. If no licence is obtainable then the law allows that up to 1% of a work may be copied for classroom use in any three-month period specified by the Act. (The Act actually lays down that these periods are fixed as 1 January to 31 March, 1 April to 30 June, 1 July to 30 September and 1 October to 31 December). These allowances may not be claimed if the person doing the copying knew, or ought to have known, that a licensing scheme was available, but no licensing scheme is allowed to restrict copying to below these very small limits.

151 Can the library do this copying on behalf of the teacher/lecturer?

Yes. But make sure the terms of the licence are known before agreeing to do such copying.

Libraries and archives

Copying published literary, dramatic or musical works

This is the most important limitation on owner's rights as far as librarians and archivists are concerned. The main user group mentioned in the Act is libraries and archives. The special exceptions for libraries and archives apply to literary, dramatic and musical works but not to artistic works.

152 Are the terms 'library' and 'archive' defined?

No. There are definitions of prescribed libraries and archives but not of libraries and archives generally.

153 Are the terms interchangeable?

No. Specific allowances are given to libraries and archives separately.

154 So what are libraries allowed to do that is special?

Quite a lot. Firstly, they can supply copies of works to their users.

Copying for users – periodicals

155 What constitutes a periodical?

This is not defined. The word 'periodical' implies some concept of being issued at periods of time. Therefore monographs in series, technical report literature and publishers' series would probably not count as periodicals as they are not linked to any timescale. A further problem could be newspapers. Although most librarians view newspapers as periodicals, some dictionaries define the word 'periodical' as excluding newspapers!

156 Is there a limit on how much of a work can be copied for a user?

Yes. There are different limits for different kinds of material. In the case of a periodical, no user can be supplied with a copy of more than one article in the same periodical issue.

157 Can the user have more than one copy of the same article?

Not under any circumstances.

158 Supposing the volume of separate issues has been bound, how does this affect copying?

The law is not specific but it seems likely that the interpretation would be that not more than one article could be copied from any one original periodical part as issued to the public. The subsequent binding by the library would, in any case, reduce the freedom to copy for the user if this view were taken as the bound volume would become the 'issue'. As this would change the amount allowed to be copied by an action beyond either the copyright owner's or the user's control, it is unlikely that this view would be taken. The original form of publication is therefore what really counts.

159 Supposing the article includes some drawings or photographs. Is it allowed to copy these as well?

Yes. If an article is copied for someone, then it is allowed to copy any accompanying illustrations. Accompanying is an important word. If the article is in, say, an art journal and is supplemented by high-quality plates of paintings just to further illustrate the artist's work, these may not be copied unless they are intrinsic to the understanding of the text.

160 What counts as an 'article'?

Unfortunately this term is defined but in very general terms. An article, in the context of an article in a periodical, means an item of any description.

161 Does this include things like advertisements, the title page, contents page or index?

Yes, so the user should not really be supplied with an article from an issue and also the contents page.

162 What about making copies of contents pages and circulating them for information amongst staff?

This is not allowed. In the first place, it is multiple copying and secondly the library cannot make copies for people unless they sign the declaration form first.

163 So is copying contents pages not allowed at all?

It would be possible to circulate one copy of the contents page amongst staff, provided one of them asked for the copy in the first place. Alternatively, it is a good idea to write to the publishers concerned and ask if they will permit this. Most say they will as it is good advertising for their journals, but some take the view that it could encourage related copying (i.e. more than one copy requested by different people at the same time for the same purpose). See also paragraph 183ff.

164 Supposing the user wants two articles from the same issue?

Only one can be provided. However, it might be possible for the user to claim fair dealing if the user borrowed the periodical issue and made the copies personally. This would then require a fair dealing defence so the copying should not be of such an extent that this was not a plausible defence.

165   If a publisher charges a higher rate for a library subscription to a periodical, can more copying be done?

No, unless the publisher has specifically stated this in the publicity, catalogues or in a specific letter to the library.

166   Can articles be copied from newspapers?

Yes. Whether the rules for copying from monographs or periodicals apply is slightly doubtful. Note also that there is a Newspaper Licensing Agency (see Section 10 on Licences).

167   But to copy one article from a newspaper often involves incidentally copying another, or at least part of another. What is the position then?

Technically only the article actually required can be copied. To be perfectly correct all other parts of the page should be blanketed! But this would be incidental copying, really as an accident or done simply in the normal process of doing what is allowed. If a case were brought, it might be possible to argue, by analogy, incidental copying similar to that allowed for artistic works in photographs (see paragraph 366) but that is only an opinion.

168   Does the copying of article extend to conference proceedings?

It will depend on the nature of the conference publication. If the conference is held regularly then it could be a periodical (annual is the most common). Conferences which are merely numbered with no indication of the timescale in which they are held will most likely be monographs (non-periodical publications).

169   What about technical reports in a numbered series?

Generally these must be treated as separate monographs.

170 Supposing the periodical issue consists of just one article?

The law specifically states that one article may be copied from a periodical issue. It seems clear that this allows the copying of an article if it constitutes the entire issue of a periodical, although any other material in that issue, such as title page, advertisements or other ephemeral material, must not be copied.

171 What about individually tailored information services?

The arrangement whereby the librarian scans various information services for material that is considered relevant to the researches of library users and then obtains copies of these items and passes them on to users without being asked for them is an infringement.

172 What can be done for researchers in this situation?

There is no reason why a librarian may not produce a current awareness bulletin from which staff select and request items they require but they must ask for items, not have them sent gratuitously. See paragraph 137ff on current awareness bulletins.

173 Supposing they are two students at a university requiring the copies for totally different courses?

This does not seem to matter. They still require them for substantially the same purpose and they are receiving instruction in the same place although this might not apply if two lecturers asked for the same material for totally different courses.

Abstracts

174 Does the abstract that goes with a journal article have a separate copyright?

Yes. It is a distinct work which can stand alone – otherwise it is not really an abstract.

175   Can any abstract be copied?

Yes, but not those which appear in abstracting services such as *Chemical Abstracts*. The law says abstracts which accompany articles in scientific or technical journals come into this exception but just what 'scientific' or 'technical' means is open for discussion.

176   Can the abstract be copied with the article?

Yes. The law states that such abstracts can be copied freely unless there is a licensing scheme which covers them, in which case you must belong to the scheme to copy the abstracts. At the time of writing no such scheme has been devised.

177   How about writing abstracts for information services?

It is quite in order to prepare abstracts from scratch by summarizing the article concerned using skill and knowledge to read the article and present the information in a different form. You should not use actual text from the original article. Once written, the copyright belongs to you or your employer as appropriate.

178   Can they be used in information bulletins?

Yes. They can be duplicated, printed, given away or sold.

Copying for users – monographs

179   What about books (monographs)?

The librarian may supply one copy of not more than a reasonable proportion of a book to a reader. The law does not use the word 'monograph' (or 'book' except in relation to Public Lending Right) but rather 'published edition other than an article in a periodical'.

180   What constitutes a 'reasonable' proportion?

This is not defined but the British Copyright Council has indicated that it views '10%' as reasonable. Although this is not a legal definition it is a helpful guideline. It seems safe to assume that a reasonable proportion is larger than a substantial part because, if less than a substantial part had been copied, there would be no need to claim any defence. Like 'substantial part' and 'fair dealing' this is a matter of individual judgment.

181 Supposing a book consists mostly of photographs and plates?

Each item will be a copyright item in its own right and must be treated as such. Libraries may not copy artistic works (such as photographs and plates) on behalf of users unless they accompany the text requested. So the library may copy illustrations accompanying material but the illustrations must accompany the text. Text which accompanies illustrations will not count for this allowance.

Restrictions on copying for users

182 Can any librarian copy for someone under these conditions?

Yes. There is no discrimination in favour of prescribed libraries in this area. See paragraph 228.

183 Are there other restrictions?

Yes. The librarian can copy an article from a periodical or part of a published work only if the user signs a declaration form which states

- that a copy has not previously been supplied
- that the copy will not be used except for research or private study and that a copy will not be supplied to any other person
- that to the best of [his] knowledge no person with whom [he] works or studies has made or intends to make at about the same time a request for substantially the same material for substantially the same purpose

- that if the declaration is false the copy becomes an infringing copy and the reader is responsible as if [he] had made the copy [him]self.

In addition, the user is required to pay a sum which will cover not only the cost of making the copy but make a general contribution towards the running of the library.

184 Those 'substantiallys' have turned up again. Are they defined in this part of the Act any better than in the other?

In a word, no. The same uncertainty applies (see paragraph 18ff).

185 Can a user really be expected to sign a statement about the intentions of other people?

No, that is not what is being asked. Users sign to say that to the best of their knowledge nobody else is going to ask for copies of substantially the same material . . . Thus the user can be in complete ignorance and truthfully sign the form.

186 Does this declaration have to be made when the request is made?

No. But it must be made before the copy is handed over. These two actions often coincide in smaller libraries, but in large libraries or public libraries there is often a waiting time between the request and the arrival of the copy. It is perfectly in order to obtain the signed declaration at the time the request is made but it must be borne in mind that in some circumstances a copy may not be supplied but the original lent instead. In this case the declaration is superfluous. On the other hand the requester may not be aware that the request will be fulfilled by a photocopy so it would be reasonable not to ask for a signature until the document was handed over.

187   What happens when requests are received by telephone or letter?

It may be possible that the request can be processed but the copies cannot be handed over until the declaration form has been signed. This may well cause rather long correspondence but there is no easy way round this.

188   Can the declaration be sent by fax?

It seems likely. Fax is widely regarded in legal circles as an adequate substitute for the actual signed document. Much larger transactions than library photocopies are settled in this way!

189   Can the declaration be made electronically rather than having to visit the library in person?

Although the Electronic Communications Act allows electronic signatures for all kinds of transactions, where legislation specifically requires a physical signature, this must be repealed. As at April 2001 this has not happened for this provision in the copyright law.

190   Must payment be made before the copies are handed over?

No, but payment must be made at some point (see paragraph 215ff).

191   What if the person making the request lives overseas?

This makes no difference. Even though the amounts may be small, payment cannot be avoided.

192   What if something is required urgently?

You need to use ingenuity but the law must be observed.

193   Is there a standard form in which this declaration must be made?

Yes. The text is published in Statutory Instrument 89/1212
Schedule 2 Form A and also at the end of this book.

194 So, as long as these conditions are met, can any librarian copy for a user?

It is not so simple. The user must sign a declaration but, in addition, the librarian must be satisfied that the requirements of two
or more people are not

* similar
* related,

and that no person is furnished with

* more than one copy
* more than one article from a periodical issue
* more than a reasonable part of any other published work.

195 How can a librarian tell if the requirements of two or more users are 'similar'?

Similar is defined only in terms of substantially the same material
at substantially the same time and for substantially the same purpose!

196 So is there really no guidance as to what these terms mean?

No. It is fairly easy to give examples of what would be regarded
as substantial as in paragraph 18ff but it is very difficult to say
what would not be regarded as substantial in these terms.

197 How can a librarian tell if requirements are 'related'?

This is a lot easier. Related is defined as 'those persons receiving
instruction to which material is relevant at the same time and

place.' This is to stop classroom copying by libraries in educational establishments.

198 Can the librarian rely on the user's honesty when signing the declaration form?

Basically, yes in respect of the purposes for which the copy is required, but certain measures to ensure the law is complied with must also be in place.

199 Supposing the user signs the declaration and it turns out to be untrue?

Librarians cannot be expected to know the inner motives of their users and the law recognizes this. The librarian may rely on a signed declaration from the reader as to the purpose for which the copy is required and the truthfulness of the statement that a copy has not been supplied by another librarian previously.

200 Then who is liable if the user signs a false declaration?

The law specifies that it is the user who would be guilty as if they had made the copy themselves.

201 How can a librarian know that a copy has not been obtained from another library?

That is not possible. But the declaration which the user signs specifically states that the user has not been supplied with a copy by you or any other librarian.

202 Can the user give the copy to someone else?

Perhaps. But the declaration says that the reader will not use the copy except for research or private study. Giving it away could be regarded as using it for other purposes but this is open to question. What is clear is that if the user gave it to someone else and they used it for any other purpose, this would make it an infringing copy. But the reader signs a declaration to say they will not give a copy of it to anyone else, i.e. they will not give a copy of the copy with which they have been supplied to anyone else. In other words, they will not photocopy the photocopy.

203 What happens if the user no longer requires the copy and subsequently gives these copies back to the library?

Unless the library considers itself a prescribed library it might be wise to refuse such generosity, although another view is that the copy is perfectly legitimate and can therefore be regarded a having the status of the original and can be given to a non-prescribed library. It would be sensible to document this, just in case its status were questioned.

204 Would it be best to destroy such copies?

Not necessarily. The user is entitled to keep the copy and may add it to files or other papers. These are often then deposited in an appropriate department of the institution or company. A suitable registry would need to be used for depositing such material but see the previous paragraph.

205 If a user gives the copy to someone else, can a user have another from the library?

No, because a user must sign to say they have not previously been supplied with a copy.

206 Supposing a user genuinely lost the previous copy?

The librarian cannot legally supply another. Readers should not be so careless! However, there seems to be nothing to stop readers borrowing the item and making a further copy for their private use. In this case, the copying would fall outside the provisions for libraries and become fair dealing.

207 What is the position if a second user also genuinely asks for the same material as the first, equally ignorant of the request by the first person?

If the librarian is aware of this, the second person cannot be supplied with a copy.

208 That seems rather unfair on the second user.

Perhaps so. But the idea is that a user should share the first person's copy.

209 Do all these references to the 'librarian' really mean only the person in charge of the library?

No. The law says that references to the librarian include a person acting on behalf of the librarian.

210 Can any librarian make a copy for any member of the public?

It would appear so although it might be difficult for a member of the general public to satisfy all the conditions if that person asked for a copy from the librarian of an industrial or commercial company.

211 What about information brokers who obtain documents from libraries for their clients?

If a broker goes to a library in person to ask for a copy to be made and that copy is for a client, the librarian should not make the copy unless the broker can produce a signed copy of the appropriate declaration form. The broker cannot sign a declaration that the document is required by the broker personally for the purposes of research or private study.

212 Could the broker be regarded as acting on behalf of the librarian?

Not really, because the broker will actually be asking the library for the copies.

213 Could the broker collect the properly signed forms on behalf of a client and bring them to the library to request copies?

This would seem a possible solution but the librarian would need to be sure that the signatures on the forms were actually those of the persons requiring the copies. Signatures of agents are not allowed.

214 Can the broker charge for the copies?

No. The broker can recoup the cost through charging for other services but not for the copy itself.

215 Must all library users pay?

Yes. All copying done on behalf of someone else by librarians must be paid for.

216 What is the point of making people pay?

Basically the idea was introduced to stop publicly funded libraries being overwhelmed by demands for free photocopies. Users enjoyed a privilege but it was not to be funded from the public purse. Unfortunately the law is so framed that the rule applies to all libraries.

217 Supposing circumstances are such that the user cannot pay?

Legally, some way must be found for payment to be made. For example, employees in a company or researchers in a university should pay when copies are made for them. They could be reimbursed by the institution later or a voucher system could be introduced but some kind of payment should be made.

218 Is the amount specified?

Not directly, but it must be a sufficient amount to not only cover the cost of making the copy but also to contribute towards the general running costs of the library.

219   Is photocopying subject to VAT?

Yes, although the amounts on individual copies may be so small that a per-page charge which is calculated to include the VAT is probably the most practicable way to collect this.

220   Do users of public libraries have to pay?

Yes. Some people have argued that the payment of local council tax is a contribution to the general expense of the library but that would only apply to residents of the authority running the library and users must still pay for the actual cost of the photocopy.

221   What about students?

They should pay like everyone else although, again, it could be argued that part of their fees is for the general upkeep of the library. Again, they still have to pay for the copies.

222   What about people in industrial and commercial companies? Can they really be expected to pay?

Yes. Payments can be made in blocks rather than at individual times but the library should raise an invoice to the user at regular intervals. Internal accounting procedures may allow this to be paid from a department within a company to the library but there is no way that payment can be avoided.

Interlibrary supply

223   The term 'supply' has been used because it is important to distinguish between lending and copying for interlibrary purposes. For lending between libraries see paragraph 317ff. Copies supplied between libraries are often referred to as 'interlibrary loans' but they are actually copies supplied for retention. It is also important to distinguish between interlibrary copying, which is intended for one library to supply copies for the collection of another library, and copying for individuals who have made their request to their own library which does not hold the material required and which has therefore transmitted the request to another library. The law makes provision for interlibrary copying but copying by one library for users of another library must be treated as a two-stage process. See the diagram below if you are confused!

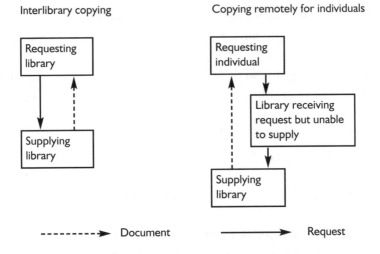

224   What about supplying copies through interlibrary arrangements for individual users?

Either the library which receives the original request must send it on to another library with the declaration form (see paragraph 183ff) or the library which receives the request must have a clear agreement with the library to which the request is sent that the first library will collect and retain the declaration form on behalf of the second library which made the copy. Otherwise the library making the copy has no proof that the copy was made legally.

225   How does the British Library Document Supply Centre (BLDSC) manage to supply copies to individuals?

Exactly as described in the previous paragraph. All institutional users of BLDSC services sign just such a declaration to act on behalf of the British Library in this respect. (See also Section 10.)

226 Which libraries can supply copies, then?

Any library in the UK can make and supply photocopies of material in its collection.

227 What about receiving copies?

Only prescribed libraries may request and receive copies for their collections.

228 What is a prescribed library?

A prescribed library is carefully defined as any library in one of the following categories not conducted for profit (see paragraph 233):

- any public library which is defined as a library administered by a library authority in England and Wales; a statutory library authority in Scotland or an Education and Library Board in Northern Ireland
- the British Library, the National Libraries of Scotland and Wales, the Bodleian Library (Oxford) and the University Library, Cambridge
- libraries in educational establishments
- Parliamentary and Government libraries
- local authority libraries
- any library whose purpose is to facilitate or encourage study of a wide range of given topics (see paragraph 232)
- any library whose purpose is to facilitate or encourage study of a wide range of given topics and which is outside the UK.

229 What constitutes an educational establishment?

Educational establishment is defined broadly as any school, college, polytechnic or university in the public sector (for specific details see SI 89/1068 and paragraph 149ff).

230   Is a government library restricted to those in Civil Service departments?

No, the definition includes any library conducted for or administered by an agency which is administered by a Minister of the Crown. So, for example, the library of a NHS hospital would count as a government library. The library of a private hospital would not.

231   What is the difference between a public library and a library administered by a local authority?

This latter category is intended for those libraries which act as libraries for departments of local or county councils. For example, many planning or environmental health departments have their own libraries and some councils have a members' library for councillors' benefit.

232   What is this 'wide range of given topics' just mentioned?

It is actually listed as 'bibliography, education, fine arts, history, languages, law, literature, medicine, music, philosophy, religion, sciences (including natural and social science) or technology'.

233   What exactly does 'conducted for profit' mean?

This is a very important phrase as it does not simply apply to the library itself but includes the organization which owns or administers the library. So the library of a major industrial company may well not be conducted for profit but the owning company certainly is and the library is therefore not a prescribed library.

234   What about charities?

The library of a charity may or may not be a prescribed library, depending on the purpose of the charity. If it is a charity whose aims are primarily to facilitate or encourage the study of the range of topics stated, then the library can claim to be prescribed. If the charity is mainly concerned with other purposes such as improving social welfare, advancing human rights or promoting particular points of view or if the charity operates commercially, then it cannot claim to be prescribed.

235 What about libraries of learned societies?

Many of these will qualify, as the primary aim of the society will be to facilitate or encourage the study of the relevant subject. But, like charities, it will depend on the aims of the society administering the library.

236 What about private libraries?

Some private libraries could say they are conducted for profit and in that case they cannot qualify but others are charitable in status and again it will depend on the nature of the charity.

237 Can anything be copied by prescribed libraries?

No. There are restrictions on both periodical articles and books (monographs).

238 What are the restrictions?

Firstly, no library may be supplied with more than one copy of any material. Secondly, no library may be supplied with a copy of more than one article from a periodical issue or even part of a non-periodical work unless the requesting library also supplies a written statement to the effect that it is a prescribed library and does not know, and has not been able by reasonable inquiry to find out the name and address of someone entitled to authorize the making of the copy. Thirdly, the requesting library must pay.

239 What does 'reasonable inquiry' mean?

This is not defined but it should be remembered that as the library which is being asked to make the copy must hold the material it is quite possible that the requesting library could obtain the required information from the supplying library and even more likely that the supplying library could find this out anyway. However, if the material is published by a company now out of business or in a remote corner of the world and the publisher does not reply to correspondence, then the copies can be made. There is always the remote chance the copyright owner might appear and challenge what has been done. Nothing is certain in the world of copyright!

240 Who is the person entitled to authorize the making of the copy?

As the requirement is to make a copy of all or a substantial part of the work, the publisher will probably be the only person who can authorize the making of such a copy as publishers usually own the copyright in the total publication (as against authors who own the content of the text, illustrators who own rights in their work, etc.). However, modern publishing contracts are usually for fixed, often short, terms, so many rights in individual parts of the monograph may have reverted to the author. However, the publisher will still own the typographical copyright.

241 Is a prescribed library allowed to keep the copies and add them to stock?

Yes. This is one way that the problem of two people requiring the same material can be overcome. Reader A borrows the photocopy and returns it. Reader B then borrows it in the same way as any other library materials.

242 What if a copy is lost or destroyed?

A second copy could possibly be asked for as prescribed libraries may only request one copy and there is no time limit on this. However, it is a nice point that, if the photocopy had been placed in the permanent collection, then the library might be able to request a replacement at some distant date as the first photocopy is legitimate and can be regarded as part of the permanent collection. See paragraph 257.

243 Can the library subsequently dispose of the copy to another library?

It seems probable that this can be done only to another pre-scribed library which did not already have a copy of the material in question, but whether this second library would also have to pay the stipulated amount is open to question.

244 Suppose the library sold off its collection. What should happen to the photocopies?

They should either be sold to another prescribed library (which should pay the cost of making the copies, plus a contribution to the running expenses of the library) or destroyed.

245 Must libraries pay for interlibrary copying?

Yes, in exactly the same way as individual users must pay libraries for copies made for them, i.e. the cost must include not only making the copy but a general contribution to the running expenses of the library.

246 Can the fees be waived?

No. This is not allowed.

247 Does payment using British Library forms fulfil this requirement?

Yes. BLDSC charges are intended to cover all the costs of a transaction and contribute to the running costs of the British Library so these meet the legal requirements.

248 Does interlibrary copying attract VAT?

Yes, just as copying for individuals does.

249 How can a library which is not a prescribed library obtain a photocopy on interlibrary loan?

Libraries that are not prescribed libraries may not request mater-ial from other libraries for their collections. Only prescribed libraries, but any individual, can request material from other libraries.

250 What can those working in industry and commerce, and other non-prescribed libraries, do for users who want copies of documents not held in their library?

Individuals are entitled to receive copies, provided they have signed the appropriate declaration form. They are entitled to receive copies from librarians (and any library in the UK is a pre-scribed library for the purposes of supplying copies) or persons acting on behalf of librarians. Therefore it would seem logical that a library user in a non-prescribed library may request a docu-ment from the librarian, who in turn requests it from another librarian, at which point the first librarian is acting on behalf of the second and supplies the copy for the use of the original user (not the librarian). Thus users can obtain a copy of a document not immediately available in their own library. An alternative is for the librarian of the prescribed library to arrange to act as an agent on behalf of the non-prescribed library to which the request will be sent for the user, but this is rather tortuous and not altogether clearly allowed. In either case the non-prescribed librarian is simply the agent (letter-box) for the prescribed library. All this is rather complex so an example might help.

Example. A researcher in Anybros Ltd asks the librarian of that company for a copy of an article from a periodical which Anybros does not take but which is taken by Sometown Univ-ersity. The librarian of Anybros cannot apply to Sometown University because the library of Anybros is not a prescribed library. So the librarian applies, acting simply as the letter-box for the researcher, who is entitled to ask for copies from Sometown University under the library provisions. The librarian of Anybros Ltd must be aware that Sometown University Library see the librarian as acting as their agent to handle requests from individu-als which are to be passed to Sometown University. This would require, if not a proper agreement, at least some kind of letter of intent and the arrangement cannot be inferred from the general situation of the Copyright Act itself. These two models are just ideas which might be allowed. There are a number of reasons why they might not but only a test case would settle the issue one way or the other.

251 Can the non-prescribed library keep the copy?

Probably not although the law is not clear. Copies can only be requested for the use of individuals and must be handed over to them but if they have then acquired legitimate status it may be possible to do with them anything that could be done with the original, which would include donating it to any kind of library. If this happens the actions should be clearly documented to show the non-prescribed library behaved properly.

252 What about brokers who request items through interlibrary loan for their clients?

The broker cannot easily do this as the broker is certainly not a prescribed library. However, the broker could simply be acting as a letter-box for the client as an individual, as mentioned in paragraph 250, or could enter into a proper agreement with a prescribed library to be their agent. Again all this is not at all clear under the Act.

253 Can the broker charge for the copies obtained through interlibrary loan?

No. This would be dealing in the copies, which is an infringement. The broker can, however, charge for other services and so recoup the costs necessarily incurred in obtaining the document through interlibrary loan.

Copying for preservation

Note that for preservation purposes archives are included in the law as well as libraries.

254   Can libraries or archives copy their own materials under these conditions?

Yes, so long as the conditions stipulated are fulfilled.

255   Can anything in a prescribed library or archive be copied?

No. Firstly, material has to be in the permanent collection of the library or archive. Therefore, it is not allowed to borrow a document from somewhere else, put it into the collection on a temporary basis, copy it and then return it to the original owner. This is particularly important for collections which are deposited for limited periods (e.g. the lifetime of the owner). Secondly, the material has to be in the permanent collection and available only for reference on the premises or for loan only to other libraries or archives. Thirdly, it must not be reasonably practicable for the librarian or archivist to purchase a copy.

256   Is it permitted to make more than one copy for preservation?

This seems unlikely. The Act says 'a copy' may be made.

257   For exactly which reasons can material be copied for preservation?

The law allows copying in order to replace an item in the permanent collection for reference purposes only so that the original can be saved from constant use, either by withdrawing it altogether or relieving the amount of use made of each copy or for replacing material in another library or archive which has been lost, damaged or destroyed. Clearly a library or archive cannot replace material in its own collection in this way since, if it is lost or destroyed, it is not there to copy!

258   Can one library or archive copy for another?

Yes, provided that the requesting library or archive provides a declaration to the effect that it is a prescribed library or archive and it has not been practicable to purchase a copy and that the copy is required as a replacement for an item in the permanent collection which has been lost, damaged or destroyed and for reference purposes only. In addition, the requesting library or archive must pay as set out in paragraph 245ff.

259 Which libraries and archives are concerned?

First, for supplying copies for preservation and replacement, any library or archive in the United Kingdom. Secondly, for requesting and receiving copies, any prescribed library or any archive not conducted for profit and not forming part of, or administered by, an organization conducted for profit. Note that for archives this is different from the limitations on libraries, which set out specific classes of library. So the archive of a charity whose primary aim was, say, social welfare, would be a prescribed archive but the library of the same charity would not. So, the archive of a major chemical company could copy material to replace that in a university library but the reverse is not true.

260 Once the material has been copied, can it be used like other materials in a library or archive?

Yes, provided that it is added to the permanent collection.

261 So what about books or periodicals in general lending collections which are falling apart or are lost?

These cannot qualify for copying under these special regulations. Replacement copies must be bought from the publisher, where available, or a copy obtained from another library if the conditions for that are met (i.e. the publisher cannot be traced and the copy cannot easily be purchased).

262 Could a prescribed library or archive obtain a copy of a work from a library if the work was in the general lending collection?

Yes, provided the copy being made was for use only in the permanent reference collection or in a collection available for lending to other libraries (but not individuals).

Copying unpublished works

263 Can unpublished materials in a library or archive be copied for users?
Yes, under certain conditions.

264 What are the conditions?
First, the work should not have been published before the document was deposited. Secondly, copying may not take place if the author has prohibited this.
Example. Edward Gotrip writes a novel in the hope he will become famous and deposits the manuscript with the local public library. Subsequently it is published. The public library is entitled to copy the manuscript even though the text has become a published novel. However, Una Suming has her book published and *then*, having become famous, deposits the manuscript with the local public library, but no copying of it is allowed.

265 Can the librarian or archivist plead ignorance of the fact that the author had prohibited copying?
Not really. The law says that copies may not be made when the author has prohibited this and the librarian or archivist knows, or ought to know, that this is the case. Therefore, it is sensible to keep a register of deposited unpublished material with notes on any items which the author has prohibited the library or archive from copying.

266 Can whole works be copied, or only parts?
The law allows copying of the whole of an unpublished document.

267 Can unpublished works be copied for anyone?

Yes, provided that the reader signs a declaration to say that the documents are required only for research or private study, that the documents were not published before they were deposited and the reader pays a sum which covers the cost of making the copy and a contribution to the general running costs of the library or archive.

268 Can they have more than one copy?

No person may have more than one copy of any work.

269 Do users have to pay?

Yes, they must pay just as in paragraph 215.

270 Do the restrictions on not supplying copies to more than one person for substantially the same purpose at substantially the same time apply?

No, these restrictions are not laid down for unpublished works.

271 Is there a standard declaration form as for published materials?

Yes. The text is published in Statutory Instrument 89/1212 Schedule 2 Form B and also at the end of this book.

272 Can copies be supplied from one archive to another?

No. Copying between archives applies only to published works and the sections on unpublished works allow only copying for individuals. It would seem likely, by analogy with a user of a non-prescribed library, that the user of a library or archive could ask that library or archive to apply on their behalf for a copy of an unpublished work but they would have to sign the appropriate declaration form, pay the required amount and also retain the copy for personal use, not present it to the library or archive which has acted as intermediary for them.

Copying as a condition of export

273   Supposing a library or archive contains material which is still in copyright but is of considerable national interest and it is decided to sell this abroad, can anything be done to copy it before it is taken out of the country?

Sometimes, yes. If the condition of export is that a copy is made to be retained in this country it is not an infringement to make the copy or to receive it to be kept in a library or archive.

Public administration

274   Are there any other reasons for being allowed to copy?

Yes. The other main reason is what the Act calls public administration.

275   What does 'public administration' cover?

Not as much as it would at first seem! Basically it covers

- Parliamentary proceedings
- judicial proceedings
- Royal Commissions
- statutory inquiry.

276   What can be copied?

There are no limits. The Act says, 'Copyright is not infringed by anything done for the purposes of Parliamentary or judicial proceedings.' The only qualification is a further allowance to the effect that if anything is copied for the proceedings and subsequently published in those proceedings this is not itself an infringement of copyright.

Material open to public inspection

277 Many libraries contain registers of various kinds and often act as a public information point for local authority activity such as planning applications or electoral registers. Can any of this material be copied?

When material is open to the public as part of a statutory requirement, or is on a statutory register, any material in it which contains factual information can be copied without infringing the copyright in it as a literary work so long as this is done with the authority of the appropriate person and copies are not issued to the public.

278 Does making a copy for a member of the public constitute 'issuing copies to the public'?

No. Making single copies for individuals in this way is outside the definition of 'issuing copies to the public'.

279 Can a member of the public copy an Electoral Register?

Yes and the limits are not set down legally although there may be physical or financial restraints to consider if large quantities are needed. Where whole registers are wanted it would be better for a reader to contact the local Registrar.

280 What constitutes factual information?

Exactly that. Anything in the material which is opinion or argument for or against a case would not be covered by this allowance.

281 Does this include maps and plans?

No. The clause is specific about literary works only.

282 Supposing someone wants to inspect some documents in this class but lives some way away and cannot come to consult the documents?

Any amount of the material may be copied for such persons provided that the appropriate person gives authorization.

283 Who is an 'appropriate person'?

An appropriate person is the person who is required to make the material open to the public or the person maintaining the register. Such persons can authorize libraries and others to make copies as described above.

284 Does this apply to maps and plans as well?

Yes. There is no restriction on the material which may be copied for those needing it sent to them to exercise their rights. However, to prevent misuse, any maps supplied for this purpose must be marked with a statement to the effect that the maps have been supplied under the Copyright Act for the purposes of consulting publicly available material and must not be further copied without permission. The full text of this statement, which must be used as it stands, is printed in SI 89/1099. (Interestingly, the Statutory Instrument refers to statutory registers but the relevant sections of the Act do not.)

285 Does this also apply to statutory registers such as registers of voters?

Apparently not, because no mention is made of statutory registers in the relevant section. However, the Statutory Instrument does refer specially to statutory registers in this section, so it is unclear just what is allowed.

286 Do these regulations apply only to UK materials?

Mostly, yes. The two exceptions are material made open to the public by the European Patent Office and the World Intellectual Property Organization, both intended to assist the process of patent registration.

287   What about material which constitutes public records?

Any material which constitutes public records under the appropriate Public Records Acts which are open to public inspection can be copied and copies supplied to anyone, with the authority of the appropriate officer as appointed under the relevant Acts of Parliament.

288   What if an Act of Parliament actually requires that something be copied for the processes of law?

If the copying is a required part of an Act of Parliament then it is not an infringement of copyright.

289   Supposing a copy is needed because of a national crisis such as war?

This may be allowed as being in the public interest. Copies were actually made for medical personnel during the Gulf War on the assumption that the Court would not permit the copyright to be defended in these circumstances.

290   Does the existence of a separate typographical copyright prevent libraries and others from copying materials?

No. the law specifically states that anything that can be done by way of copying with a copyright work can also be done to the typographical layout of that work.

Issuing copies to the public

291   Is issuing copies to the public the same as publishing?

No, issuing copies to the public is much wider in scope. As well as publishing it includes rental and lending.

292   If issuing copies to the public is an infringement, how can libraries offer a lending service?

The law makes it clear that the right to issue copies to the public only applies to works not previously put into circulation in the EEA. There are specific provisions for the lending and rental of copyright material (see 'lending and rental' under each type of material).

293   Does this idea of issuing copies to the public have any bearing on acquisition of materials?

Essentially, no. Any responsibility for infringing importation would rest with the bookseller involved, not the library. Libraries occasionally import single copies but these are not for commercial purposes so infringement is unlikely.

Performing a work

294   Libraries and archives are not often involved in public performances. Is this really important for them?

Libraries are increasingly involved in cultural activities and some have library theatres so it is important to be aware of the owner's rights, especially when library materials may be utilized to put on performances. This includes plays, concerts and arts festivals generally.

295   Can only the copyright owner authorize performance?

Yes although it may be done through a licensing agency (see Section 10).

296   Does performance mean just plays or presentations?

No. Performance includes delivery of speeches, lectures or sermons and also includes presentation by visual or audible means.
Example. If the library possesses some poems by a local author, they may not be copied. But it is also an infringement to recite them in public or make a video of someone reciting them in public. Family videos of weddings, for example, may infringe the copyright in the vicar's sermon if read from a prepared text.

However, if the vicar is speaking extempore, there is no copyright in the sermon until it has been recorded (on the video). The vicar then owns the copyright in the sermon and the person who shot the video owns the copyright in the video as such!

297   Does this mean that poems cannot be used for public recitation?

Not quite. One person may read a reasonable extract from a copyright work in public provided that the reading is accompanied by sufficient acknowledgement.

298   What do the terms 'reasonable extract' and 'sufficient acknowledgement' mean?

They are not defined. Reasonable extract is a matter of judgment. Sufficient acknowledgement would certainly mean saying who wrote the work, when and where it was published, if published at all.

299   What about story-telling for children in libraries?

Technically this is an infringement by performance (see Section 10).

300   Sometimes teachers want to perform plays or hold concerts using copyright library materials. Is this allowed?

Yes, provided that only pupils, teachers and other persons directly connected with the educational establishment are present. This does not include mums and dads!

Broadcasting a work

301   Does this have any implications for libraries and archives?

As far as literary, dramatic or musical works go, the main fact to bear in mind is that broadcasting a work is an infringement of the owner's rights. So if a local radio station wished to use some of the library's holdings for broadcasting purposes, such as poems, musical compositions or extracts from local history material, this would not be allowed without permission. This would not apply if the use were solely for news reporting.

Adaptation

302 Does adaptation apply just to plays, novels or similar materials?

No. It includes translation, adaptation, conversion of dramatic works to non-dramatic works and turning a story into a cartoon or similar work. Translating a work is considered an adaptation and translations should not be made without due consideration for the purpose for which they are made and the use to which they will be put.

303 What can be done for a researcher in a laboratory who needs a technical article translated?

Provided the translation was entirely for the use of the researcher, fair dealing (see paragraph 121ff) could be claimed, but if numerous copies of the translation were made then this would be an infringement. Certainly copies of the translation could not be sold.

304 What about a student who wants to translate a play in a foreign language?

If the student makes his or her own translation there is unlikely to be a problem as copying by non-mechanical means in the course of instruction is permitted (see paragraph 142ff). It would be interesting to test the exception if an automatic translating programme were used!

Dramatic/non-dramatic works

305 It is an infringement to rewrite a non-dramatic work as a dramatic one and vice-versa. It is also an infringement to reproduce a story in another form such as pictures.

Example. Someone decides to rework Alan Ayckbourne's *Norman Conquests* as a novel. This is an infringement. Equally it would be an infringement to produce a dramatic version of one of Catherine Cookson's novels.

306 Does this restriction include turning a story into pictures, such as for a children's library?

Yes. The law specifies that it is not allowed to turn the story into a version wholly or mainly told in the form of pictures suitable for reproduction in a book, newspaper or magazine. Although this is obviously aimed at the cartoon market, it has implications for children's libraries and school libraries as well.

307 How does this affect arrangements of musical works?

Any arrangement or transcription of a musical work counts as an adaptation.

308 Does 'translation' extend to computer languages?

Yes. The law specifically states that changing a program from one computer language to another is an infringement unless this is done incidentally during the running of the program. But see Section 9.

309 Supposing an adaptation or translation has been made quite legally. Does that also attract copyright?

Yes, and the person who made the adaptation has rights in the adaptation just as the author has in the original work.

Lending and rental

Under the 1988 Act lending and rental of certain materials became an exclusive right of the copyright owner. Since 1996 this right has been extended to all materials. However, the rules are quite complicated and libraries have certain specific provisions listed.

310   What is actually meant by 'lending'?

The meaning of lending is defined in the new legislation as follows:

- that a work is made available for use on the presumption that it will, or may be, returned
- the lending does not lead to any economic or commercial advantage to the lender
- the lending is done by an establishment that is accessible to the public
- OR by a prescribed library (see paragraph 228ff) that is not conducted for profit
- BUT by a public library only if the work is covered by the Public Lending Right Act or was acquired before 1 December 1996.

Lending does not include:

- making available for public performance
- performing in public
- broadcasting
- making available for exhibition purposes
- on-the-spot reference use
- making available between establishments accessible to the public.

311   Does this mean that a library lending material cannot charge?

No. The necessary operating costs of the lending establishment may be recovered. Where lending takes place in these conditions it is not defined as 'lending'!

312   What does 'on-the-spot' mean?

This is not defined but it would seem clear that use of a work within a library or similar collection where the work is not taken out of the room would clearly be on-the-spot. Whether taking a work from one room in a building to another or from one building to another within a single site still constitutes 'on-the-spot' is not clear. It seems unlikely that 'the spot' would be stretched to use on a different site.

313   Which libraries can lend material?

Any prescribed library (see paragraph 228ff for a definition of this term) that is not conducted for profit can lend copyright works. As lending is defined as not being for economic or commercial gain, charging for this lending should not cost more than the operating costs to carry out the action. There are special restrictions for lending by public libraries.

314   What can public libraries lend?

After 1 December 1996 public libraries can lend:

*   any printed materials obtained before 1 December 1996.
*   materials acquired after 1 December 1996 that are covered by the Public Lending Right Scheme or that would have been eligible for coverage by the scheme because of their form but are precluded because of country of origin, date of the author's death, or other similar reasons.

To try to clarify this, a new edition of a book by an author who died over 70 years ago is not eligible for PLR but would have been if the author had died recently. To avoid the situation where the public library could not lend this book because it is outside the PLR scope, it can be treated as if it is eligible for lending even though it is not!

315   What about books without authors such as directories or bibliographies?

These can be for reference only if acquired after 1 December 1996.

316   What about periodicals, maps, or photographs?

If acquired after 1 December 1996 they must be for reference only.

Interlibrary loan

317   What about lending works through interlibrary loan?

Care may be needed here. Lending between establishments, which are accessible to the public, is not counted as lending. BUT there are specific clauses dealing with libraries that will probably override this general exception – normal practice is that where specific regulations exist they take precedence over general rules.

318   Can any library take part in interlibrary lending arrangements?

It depends whether the library is being asked for copies or is asking for copies and whether the library wishes to lend or borrow.

319   Which libraries can lend to other libraries?

There is no legislation that deals directly with lending between libraries. 'Lending' is defined as not including 'making available between establishments which are accessible to the public' but (a) the term 'accessible to the public' is not defined, and (b) there are separate clauses for lending from libraries which are not just establishments accessible to the public. However, some possible situations in which interlibrary loan can take place can be deduced.

320 What about libraries in commerce and industry?

As the law stands a library in this category cannot lend any material but it might be able to borrow from other libraries. However, it would not be able to lend the material borrowed as such libraries are not allowed to lend.

321 What about other libraries?

Any library which is a prescribed library (see paragraph 228ff) and which is not conducted for profit can lend material, so presumably it can be lent to other libraries.

322 What about public libraries?

As public libraries can lend only books within the Public Lending Right scheme they can lend only these items to other libraries.

323 If a work has been borrowed by a library can it then be lent to the end-user?

It would seem that this will depend on whether that library can lend this type of material to end-users from its own collection. If lending from its own collection would not be allowed it is unlikely that it could lend material from another collection. For example, public libraries cannot lend issues of periodicals so it would seem unlikely that a public library could borrow a back issue from another library (say an educational library) and lend that to the end-user when it cannot lend the same type of material from its own collection.

324 What constitutes rental?

Rental is making something available for a limited time on the expectation that it will be returned and for which a charge above the necessary operating costs is recovered.

325 Can libraries have rental schemes?

Only with the agreement of the copyright owner.

Publication right

326 What is publication right?

Publication right is a new right introduced on 1 December 1996. It is similar to, but distinct from, copyright as such.

327 Does publication right exist in all works?

No, but it can exist in any literary, dramatic, musical, or artistic work or a film.

328 So when does it exist?

Publication right exists when anyone in the EEA first publishes a work which

- is out of copyright
- is published by someone who is an EEA citizen, and published in the EEA
- has not previously been published in the UK or any EEA state.

329 Does 'published' mean published commercially?

No, in the context of publication right (and the definition is different in different contexts) it means communication to the public (an undefined term) and in particular:

- issue of copies to the public
- making the work available by means of an electronic retrieval system
- rental or lending of copies to the public
- performance, showing or exhibiting in public
- broadcasting, including cable.

330   When does an unpublished work go out of copyright?

See paragraph 78ff for details, but note that unpublished literary, dramatic and musical works of which the author had died before 1 January 1969 are protected for 50 years from the date when the new law came into force and therefore do not come out of copyright until 2039, the first date on which publication right for these classes of works can come into force. Unpublished works of which the author died after 31 December 1968 enjoy the usual 70 years protection unless the author is a national of a non-EEA country, in which case copyright lasts for as long as that country provides protection.

331   Does this mean that, where publication right comes into force, libraries and archives lose control of unpublished material in their collections?

Fortunately, no. The publication can take place only with the consent of the owner of the physical material in which the work is recorded. So a library or archive could refuse to allow a work to be published or permit this only under strict conditions (including royalties!).

332   Are there any works which may be subject to publication right now?

Possibly. It is arguable that works which existed before they were covered by legislation and which have never been published might never have been in copyright and therefore could be eligible for this new right, which applies only to works in which copyright has expired.

Artistic works

Definition

333 What is the definition of an artistic work?

The definition of artistic works includes:

- graphic works such as paintings, drawings, diagrams, maps, charts and plans, engravings, lithographs, etchings or wood-cuts
- sculpture
- collage
- photographs (including slides and negatives as well as micro-forms)
- architectural works (including buildings of any kind)
- works of artistic craftsmanship such as jewellery or pottery.

334 Does a slide count as a photograph?

Yes. Slides are protected in the same way as photographs.

335 Are overhead transparencies (OHPs) protected by copyright?

This depends on whether they contain original material prepared by the lecturer or if they are simply copies of something that already existed such as a table from a book. In the former case they might be copyright if the work is original enough. Otherwise they are another type of photograph, although when they are made on a photocopying machine it would seem equally possible to argue they are merely photocopies on a different medium.

336 Do microforms qualify for copyright?

Certainly. A microfilm or microfiche ('microforms' for short) is a photograph and attracts copyright in the same way as a photograph itself. A microform containing several different documents may also be a database (see Section 9).

337 What happens if the work which has been microfilmed is still in copyright?

There are then two copyrights, one in the original document and one in the microform. To make the new copy would require the consent of the original copyright owner.

338 Supposing the work that has been microfilmed is out of copyright?

There is probably still copyright in the microform as a photograph even though the work photographed is out of copyright. Some authorities argue that there is no copyright in the photograph of a 'flat' object such as a document but others would argue that change of medium (from paper to photograph) requires sufficient skill to create a new original work. There is no clear-cut evidence either way and case law is inconclusive.

Example. A microform of *Magna Carta* would attract copyright as a photograph but the Magna Carta certainly would not.

339   What is the situation if enlargements are made from the microform?

The enlargements can be an infringement of microform *and* the original document (if the original is still in copyright), or of just the microform if that is still in copyright but the document filmed is not.

340   Supposing a library wishes to make microform copies of works in its collection to preserve them?

This is in order only if the original documents are out of copyright or if they come under the special provisions for preservation (see paragraph 254ff) .

Ownership of copyright

341   Who owns the copyright in an artistic work?

Ownership of the copyright of an artistic work is defined in the same terms as for a literary, dramatic or musical work (see paragraph 24ff).

342   Who owns the copyright in a collection of slides?

Each slide has its own copyright just like the articles in periodical (see paragraph 34ff). However, there will also be a copyright in a compilation made up of slides. It may also be a database (see Section 9), depending on the way the collection is put together.

343   If a library or archive makes its own microforms, who owns the copyright?

The copyright belongs to the library or archive. However, if the library/archive commissions an outside bureau to do the filming, ownership of the copyright will depend on the contract between the two parties. Where the microforms have been bought from a commercial company, the copyright will remain with that company, despite the status of the original documents filmed.

344 Quite often copies of photographs supplied by libraries or archives state that, although they are old, the copyright is owned by the library or archive, from whom permission must be sought to make copies or publish the photograph. Is this legal?

The position is that the library or archive owns the photographs but not usually the copyright in them. They may well impose restrictions on the subsequent use of the photographs and that is their right as owners of the physical photographs. But they do not own the copyright in these works. If conditions are imposed, such as payment for publication, then, once these are met, the library or archive has no further claim on the photograph and certainly not the copyright in it. See also paragraph 326ff.

Definition of author

345 Who counts as the author of an artistic work?

The author of an artistic work is defined in the same terms as for a literary, dramatic or musical work (see paragraph 53ff). This includes, in the case of photographs, the photographer.

346 Do authors of artistic works have moral rights?

Yes. They are described in paragraph 21ff. Note that authors of paintings have the right to be named as the author if the work is exhibited in public. This right has to be asserted before the exhibition takes place to be valid.

Duration of copyright

347 How long does copyright in artistic works last?

Although artistic works are protected in the same way as literary, dramatic or musical works there are some important differences. Some of the rules are repeated here for ease of reference. The rules about extended and revived copyright described in paragraph 35ff also apply to artistic works.

348   Do the rules about works originating in the EEA (see paragraph 70ff) also apply?

Yes the rules in this area are the same. To save unnecessary repetition the term '70 years' has been used in the following paragraphs but marked * to remind you that the EEA/non-EEA rules apply.

Published works

349   Most published artistic works are protected for 70* years from the end of the year in which the author died with the following exceptions.

350   Anonymous/pseudonymous artistic works

Essentially copyright in these works lasts 70* years from the end of the year in which they were created, but, if published during that period, then 70* years from the end of the year in which they were first made available to the public.

351   Is 'first made available to the public' the same as 'published'?

No. In the case of artistic works it includes:

- exhibition
- included in a broadcast or cable television programme
- included in a film.

352   Published engravings

If published after the artist's death and before 1 January 1969 then engravings are protected until the year of publication + 50 years. Otherwise they are protected until the year of the artist's death + 70* years.

Unpublished works

353 Unpublished works with an author

Works of which the creator has died before 1 January 1969 and were unpublished on 1 August 1989 are protected until 2039. All other works are protected for 70* years from the end of the year in which the author died.

354 Unpublished anonymous/pseudonymous works

Works created after 1 January 1969 are protected for 70* years from the end of the year in which they were created or from being first made available to the public. However, where a work was created before 1 August 1989 copyright protection must last until 2039 regardless of the assumed date of creation.

355 Unpublished engravings

If unpublished and the artist died before 1 January 1969 then engravings are protected until 31 December 2039. Otherwise protected from the year of the artist's death + 70* years.

356 Photographs

Photographs formerly had a very complex set of rules governing expiry of copyright but the term of protection has now been standardized at the year of the photographer's death plus 70* years or, if anonymous, 70* years from creation, or, if made available to the public, 70* years from the end of the year in which that took place.

357 How long is a microform protected then?

If the author can be established, for 70* years from the year of the author's death; otherwise 70* years from the year in which the microform was made available to the public.

358   Crown and Parliamentary copyright

Where copyright in an artistic work (other than an engraving or photograph) is owned by the Crown and the work was made before 1 August 1989, copyright expires 50 years from the end of the year in which the work was created. Works made after this date are subject to the same rules as literary works (see paragraphs 67ff and 78ff). Copyright in published engravings made before 1 August 1989 expires 50 years from the year of publication. Copyright in an unpublished engraving made before 1 August 1989 expires on 31 December 2039. However, in the case of unpublished photographs, copyright in those taken on or after 1 August 1989 will last for 125 years subject to their not being published commercially within the first 75 years; those taken on or after 1 June 1957 but before 1 August 1989 would have protection until the end of 2039; and those taken before 1 June 1957 will have protection for 50 years from the end of the year in which they were taken.

Copying artistic works

359   Owner's rights

The owner has the same rights as for literary, dramatic or musical works (q.v.). Note that exhibiting a work is not a right the copyright owner enjoys, despite general belief to the contrary.

360   What about taking photographs?

A photograph of an artistic work (say, a statue or painting) is an infringement of the artist's copyright unless the work is architectural, a sculpture or a work of artistic craftsmanship and is on permanent public display in a public open space or premises open to the public.

361   What constitutes 'open to the public'?

This is not defined but it would certainly be a street or thoroughfare and any building to which the public had access in the normal course of events. Presumably a library, museum or art gallery is open to the public, although particular parts of it may not be, so these would not count (e.g. strong rooms, vaults, closed stacks, etc.). Rooms in town halls and other similar buildings are more difficult to define.

362   What constitutes 'permanent'?

Unfortunately this is not defined. Obviously something on loan for, say, six months, could not be permanent. Something might be on display for six months and then taken away and be counted as permanent because it was intended to be so when it was put on display in the first place.

363   The owners of some buildings charge copying fees to photograph artistic works housed in them even though the works must surely be out of copyright. Is this allowed?

This is not a copyright fee but a copying fee. The owners of a cathedral, for example, cannot claim there is copyright in a medieval painting but this does not stop them from charging for the privilege of access to photograph their property. The painting is their property even though the copyright has long since expired.

364   What about making a slide, OHP or microform of a painting?

Photocopying, microfilming or making a transparency or slide of a drawing, engraving or painting are all infringements.

365   What about making a model of something in a painting?

It is also an infringement to make a three-dimensional model of a picture, photograph or painting in just the same way as photographing a statue.

366 What happens if a photograph (or television programme) happens to include a piece of copyright material in the background – say, an interview in front of a recent painting in a gallery?

Incidental copying of this nature is not an infringement – but it would be if the photographer or TV producer deliberately included the painting.

367 Supposing the library/archive holds a painting which it wishes to reproduce as a slide, poster or postcard?

If the painting is out of copyright there is no problem, or if the picture is of a statue or something similar on permanent public display then there is no problem. Remember the slide, poster or postcard will attract copyright, which will be owned by the photographer or the library/archive depending on whether the photographer was an employee of the library/archive or the library/archive simply commissioned the taking of the photograph!

368 Supposing there is an exhibition of children's work and the library wants to use this for publicity material or to publish it?

Technically the copyright belongs to the children individually and the permission of the child or guardian is necessary before works can be reproduced. Some teachers might argue that the copyright belongs to the school but the child is not employed there (at least not in the sense of gainful employment!) and the teacher cannot claim the copyright because the child actually did the painting.

Fair dealing

369 Are artistic works subject to fair dealing?

Artistic works are subject to fair dealing in a similar way to literary, dramatic and musical works but there are some differences.

370 What constitutes fair dealing in an artistic work?

This is undefined as for other works. However, the same general rules apply (see paragraph 115ff).

371 Do the reasons for fair dealing – research or private study, criticism or review, and reporting current events – still apply to artistic works?

Yes. The reasons are just the same except in the area of reporting current events.

Research or private study

372 How can something be copied fairly when it is an artistic work? Surely the whole of the work would be copied?

Perhaps. Fair dealing does not exclude copying all of the work. *Example.* An art student needs to study the different ways of portraying Hercules. The student could take photographs of modern statues, paintings and drawings for personal use to carry out the research. The photographs must not be sold or published or they would not constitute fair dealing for the purposes of research. If they were subsequently sold or published this would be an infringement as they would not be fair dealing copies and might be in direct competition with the commercial exploitation of the work by the owner (such as producing postcards).

373 What about people who go to art galleries (and libraries) and make paintings of other people's paintings?

This would be considered as fair because it is for private study. The copy would have had sufficient original input from the copying painter to qualify for copyright protection in its own right but might still be challenged as an infringement of the copyright in the original work.

374   Can a student include a copy of an artistic work, say a photograph of a statue, in a thesis?

Yes. This is for research and is also providing the answer to an examination, so it is covered by educational copying. But if the thesis is published then the copyright in the artistic work is infringed.

Reporting current events

375   Can artistic works be used to report current events?

Yes, but photographs may not be used for this purpose.

376   Can artistic works be used in criticism or review?

Artistic works may be reproduced for criticism or review provided that there is sufficient acknowledgement of their authorship.

377   What constitutes sufficient acknowledgement?

This is not defined but would presumably include the name of the author at least.

378   Can an artistic work be reproduced in a journal article?

Only if the purpose is criticism or review. Simply to include a photograph of a copyright painting to illustrate a point about modern art would not be sufficient justification.

379   What about using a painting or photograph of a piece of sculpture to advertise an exhibition?

This would not be allowed.

380   What about sale catalogues which include photographs of copyright materials?

That is allowed. There is a specific clause allowing the copying of works to advertise them for sale.

Educational copying

381   May artistic works be copied for educational purposes?

Artistic works may be copied by either the teacher or the pupils themselves so long as a reprographic process is not used.

Example. A teacher or student could make their own copy of a map by drawing it themselves but must not photocopy it.

382   What about examination questions?

Anything may be done for setting questions or answering them so there are no restrictions in this area.

383   What about educational licensing schemes?

See Section 10.

384   What is to be done for the classroom teacher who wants multiple copies of, say, a photograph for classroom use?

This is not permitted. However, each student might claim fair dealing to make their own copy for research or private study purposes.

385   Can a slide be included in, say, a film or video?

No. That is copying just like any other form of copying.

386   Can an OHP be made of a work for classroom use.

Not without infringing the copyright, although the publishers have indicated they would not regard this as an infringement if a single copy from an illustration were made provided the source was acknowledged.

387   Can slides or photographs be made of artistic works for classroom use or teaching?

Not without infringing copyright or obtaining a licence.

388 Can copies be made of maps for classroom use?

Photocopies for classroom use cannot be made except under the licence of the copyright owner. Teachers and pupils may copy maps out of atlases by hand or through tracing paper as this is not a reprographic process.

Library and archive copying

See also Section 10.

389 Can libraries and archives copy artistic works in their collections in the same way as printed materials?

No. The special provisions for library and archive copying do not apply to artistic works at all.

390 What is to be done for a reader who wants a copy of a photograph?

Readers may borrow the item and copy it for themselves if they think that would be fair but the librarian is not allowed to copy on behalf of the reader. However, as fair dealing is not defined in law, it might be possible to argue that the librarian can copy for users under fair dealing provided they are certain that multiple copies are not supplied.

391 What about copying maps for users?

Under copyright law this is not permitted. Users may make their own copies under fair dealing arrangements. But see Section 10 relating to Ordnance Survey.

392 What about licences issued by publishers such as Ordnance Survey?

These are really a contract between the library and the copyright owner who is allowing the library to do certain things the law does not. As owners of the copyright Ordnance Survey (or any other publisher) are entitled to do anything they wish with their property! Failure to observe the conditions of such a licence is a breach of contract as well as an infringement of copyright. See also Section 10.

393 Supposing an article in a periodical is accompanied by a photograph?

This can safely be copied as the act makes it clear that accompanying materials can legitimately be copied, whether or not they are artistic works as such. But the photograph cannot be copied by itself – only as part of the article.

394 Are libraries allowed to supply copies of artistic works through interlibrary copying?

No.

395 What if a library or archive has lost its copy of an artistic work. Can a replacement be obtained from another library or archive?

No. Copying for preservation or replacement is restricted to literary, dramatic or musical works.

396 Can artistic works be copied as condition of export?

Like literary works, an article of cultural or historical importance may be copied if a condition of the export is that a copy be made and deposited in an appropriate library or archive.

397 Material open for public inspection

No specific mention is made of material open to public inspection of artistic works. For maps, however, see paragraph 284.

398 Can artistic works be copied for public administration purposes?

Yes, the same wide allowances apply to artistic works as to literary works.

399   Issuing copies to the public

This is restricted as for literary, dramatic and musical works (q.v.).

Performing a work

400   Is it an infringement to perform an artistic work?

There is no performing right, including the right of exhibition, for artistic works.

401   Can the owner of a painting or other artistic work put it on public display?

Yes. The right of display is not one of the acts restricted by copyright. Once the work has been purchased the owner of the work may display it but this does not alter the rights of the copyright owner to reproduce the work, e.g. on postcards, photographs, slides, etc. (see also publication right). But see paragraph 351 for the impact on duration of copyright.

Broadcasting a work

402   Supposing a television programme included a shot of a painting or sculpture. Would this be counted as broadcasting?

Yes, unless it was incidentally included as mentioned in paragraph 366. However, if the programme were about a particular painter whose works were still in copyright, then the inclusion would be deliberate and would infringe the artist's copyright. There might still be a defence of using the image for criticism or review but it would depend on the nature of the programme.

403   Supposing the television programme is a news item about an artist who has just died?

Then to include one of the artist's paintings as part of the news might not be an infringement because this would be reporting current events (see paragraph 137ff).

Adaptation

404   Is there a right of adaptation in artistic works? How does it work?

Most forms of adaptation are really copying. For example, to make a model of a painting is really an adaptation of the original to a different form as mentioned under 'models' (paragraph 365).

Lending and rental

405   Are artistic works subject to lending and rental restrictions?

Yes.

406   Does this mean that libraries may no longer lend artistic works?

Not altogether. In the first place, this restriction applies only to material acquired on or after 1 December 1996. Secondly, lending (i.e. charging no more than operational costs) is allowed for any library except a public library.

407   Why are public libraries excluded?

Because the Act specifically states that public libraries, whether or not a charge is made, cannot lend these materials, except those acquired before December 1996, or under licence.

408   Supposing there is no licensing scheme available?

The Secretary of State has the power to implement a scheme subject to appropriate payment as determined by the Copyright Tribunal if necessary.

Publication right

409   Does publication right apply to artistic works?

Yes (see paragraph 326ff).

Sound recordings

Definition

410 What is the definition of a sound recording?

The definition of a sound recording is not limited in any way by format. It is any form of recording of sounds from which sounds may be reproduced. So it includes wax cylinders, vinyl discs, audio cassettes, compact discs and DVDs. It also includes sounds recorded and stored in digital form from which sounds can be reproduced.

Authorship

411 Who is the author of a sound recording?

The producer.

412 Does the producer of a sound recording enjoy moral rights?

No (in a word!).

413 Who counts as the producer?

This term is defined as the 'person by whom the arrangements necessary for the making of the sound recording are made'.

Ownership of copyright

414 Who owns the copyright in a sound recording? Is it owned by the record company that produced the disc?

It is very important to distinguish between the copyright in the sound recording and the copyright in the material recorded.

Examples. A recording of a song by the Beatles will have all sorts of copyrights – the song, the music, the arrangement and the performance. In addition, there is a copyright in the actual sound recording which is quite separate. Similarly, an interview for an oral history project will have a copyright in what the person said, which will belong to the person interviewed. There will also be a copyright in the recording made of that interview, which will be owned by the person who made the arrangements for making the recording. Again, a recording of Beethoven's Fifth Symphony will have a copyright in the recording although there is no longer any copyright in the music a such. (NB. This is important outside libraries as the law now says it is not an infringement of the copyright in a sound recording to play it in organizations such as youth clubs. This applies only to the recording and not to the music or words of the recording.)

415 Who owns the copyright in an interview?

This is important for oral history and similar archives. The speaker owns the copyright in what is said but there is no copyright in the material until it has been recorded. Once it has been recorded the speaker owns the copyright in what has been said but the person making the recording owns the copyright in the sound recording as such. If the interview is transcribed then the person making the transcription may also be entitled to copyright in their transcription.

416 Is it necessary to get permission to make such recordings for archives?

It is advisable to obtain the permission of the speaker when the recording is made. Such permission should stipulate for what purposes the recording will be used, especially if it may be used later by a radio programme or television station. See the Oral History Society website for more information: **www.essex.ac.uk/ sociology/ohs/copyright.html.**

Duration of copyright

417 How long does copyright in a sound recording last?

Essentially 50 years from the year in which the sound recording was made or, if, it was released during that period, 50 years from the end of the year in which it was released.

418 Does 'released' mean published?

Not quite. Released means not only published in the usual sense but also if the sound recording is played in public, broadcast or included in a cable television programme. This is important for sound archive material which is lent to broadcasting organizations. The transmission of the material will mean it has been published or released and the copyright in it will expire 50 years from that time rather than 50 years from when it was made.

419 Do sound recordings have extended and revived copyright?

No. Duration of sound recordings is not linked to a human being so the period was not extended as for some other works.

Owner's rights

420 What rights does the copyright owner have?

Essentially the owner has the same rights as for literary, dramatic, musical or artistic works.

421 To copy the work

The copyright owner has the exclusive right to make copies of the work.

422 Does this include copying from one medium to another?

Yes. To make a copy of a vinyl disc onto a tape is, of course, copying the work.

423 Supposing the medium on which the work is stored is obsolete? Can copies be made onto a usable type of equipment?

Not without permission or infringing copyright.

Fair dealing

424 Is there fair dealing in sound recordings?

Only for very restricted purposes. See the individual headings below.

425 Research or private study

There is no fair dealing in sound recordings for the purposes of research or private study.

426 What can be done for a student who needs a copy of a sound recording for study purposes?

There is no legal way that such a copy can be provided. The only thing to do is to obtain permission from the copyright owner.

Reporting current events

427 Can sound recordings be used for reporting current events?

Yes. Short extracts from appropriate recordings can be used for news items and there is no need to acknowledge their source.

Criticism and review

428   Can sound recordings be used for criticism or review?

Yes, so long as the source is acknowledged. So a broadcast which includes short extracts from sound recordings to provide comment on the work of a singer or composer is allowed.

Library and archive copying

429   Can libraries and archives copy sound recordings?

No. The provisions for copying in libraries and archives are for literary, dramatic and musical works only. Remember a 'musical work' is the score as written or printed, not a sound recording of it!

430   Can a library or archive copy sound recordings for preservation purposes?

Unfortunately, no. Again, these allowances are for literary, dramatic or musical works only (but see paragraph 629ff on changes to legal deposit).

431   What can be done if a record or tape is deteriorating rapidly and will be lost if it is not copied?

Legally, nothing if it is still in copyright. If the owner can be traced, permission can be sought but otherwise the library or archive may take a risk and produce a substitute copy. It is a matter of fine judgment whether the original copyright owner would take action if this were discovered.

432   What happens if someone wishes to record a folksong for an archive?

There are special rules for this. In the first place the song must be of unknown authorship and be unpublished – in other words, a real original folksong. If this really is the case then a recording can be made, so long as the performer does not prohibit this.

433 Can the recording be kept in any local history archive?

Not initially. Only certain designated archives can maintain collections of these items.

434 Which archives are these?

There are quite a number of them but they are all national in character. There is a complete list in SI 98/1012.

435 Can copies be made from these recordings?

Yes, provided that the archivist is satisfied that they are for research or private study only and not more than one copy is supplied to any one person.

436 Is there the usual requirement that they must be paid for?

Surprisingly, no. No mention is made of payment.

437 Can they make copies for other archives?

Not under copyright law. They may have other agreements with production companies which allow this.

Educational copying

438 Is copying for educational purposes allowed?

Only in two specific cases (and one is very specific indeed). Copying for examinations is allowed (see paragraph 144) and copying for the purposes of giving instruction in the making of films or film soundtracks is allowed provided it is done by the person giving the instruction.

Copying as a condition of export

439 Do the special arrangements for copying materials of historic or cultural importance before export apply to sound recordings?

Yes. If the condition of export is that a copy is made and deposited in a library or archive, then this is not an infringement and the library or archive can make the copy, or receive the copy made elsewhere.

Material open to public inspection

440   Do the special conditions about copying such material apply to sound recordings?

It is not very likely that this would arise but the appropriate person may make copies either for use by persons who cannot exercise their statutory rights by consulting the material in person or if the material contains information of general scientific, technical commercial or economic interest. Copies may not be made for persons consulting it in person.

Public administration

441   Can sound recordings be copied for judicial proceedings, Parliamentary proceedings and statutory inquiries, as in the case of literary works?

Yes. There is no restriction in this case.

442   Issuing copies to the public

This is an exclusive right of the owner.

443   Performing the work

The owner has the exclusive right to perform the work.

444   Does this mean that if a library has a collection of sound recordings and wishes to put on a public performance of them, this is not allowed?

This can be done either with non-copyright material (i.e. too old to be protected) or with material in which the library or archive holds the copyright or if the library is covered by a Performing Rights Licence. (See Section 10.)

445 Supposing the library or archive holds oral history recordings, can these be played publicly?

Only if the library/archive owns the copyright in both the words spoken and the sound recording itself.

446 How can the library or archive obtain the copyright in the actual words spoken?

This is best done by way of an agreement with the interviewee at the time of the interview. Failure to do this could lead to infringement of the speaker's copyright.

447 If the library has a collection of sound recordings, can they be played on the library's premises?

They can be played for private listening in carrels or somewhere similar provided that not more than one person has access to the same recording at the same time, otherwise this could be considered a public performance. Otherwise they can be played only if the library (or the library authority) has a Performing Rights Licence which covers that building. Outside these limitations, public playing of copyright material is an infringement. Check with the administration to see if the library is covered by such a licence. This also applies to films, videos, television broadcasts and radio.

448 Broadcasting the work

This is an exclusive right of the copyright owner.

449 Presumably libraries and archives do not have to worry about restrictions on broadcasting?

Not true. There is an increasing interest in local studies and live comments from the past, as well as folk music and recent broadcast interviews. Where this material has been prepared, recorded or given to the library or archive, it may well be in demand from local or national broadcasting stations. To allow this to be used in this way is an infringement unless the original owner gave express permission when the recording was made.

450 Adaptation

This is an exclusive right of the owner.

Lending and rental

451 As this right includes lending as well as rental, does this mean that lending services for audio materials are not allowed?

Basically, yes. Sound recordings may not be rented to the public without the copyright owner's permission. They can be lent by prescribed libraries (see paragraph 310ff) provided the fee charged only covers the cost of administration but they cannot be lent by public libraries without a licence of some kind. See Section 10.

452 Supposing a work is held by a library in both printed form and as, say, an audiocassette. What is the position then?

This causes an anomaly. The printed book may be subject to Public Lending Right but the audiocassette is controlled by the licensing scheme offered by the producers of audio materials, probably through the BPI (British Phonographic Industries) licence. There are currently plans to introduce a separate licence for spoken word materials through the Spoken Word Publishers Association (SWPA). There is a further anomaly in that the money for the Public Lending Right royalty comes from the government and goes to the author, while any money which may be generated by the audio licensing scheme (if there is one) is paid by the library and will probably go to the producer of the cassette.

453 Does this mean that libraries may no longer lend records?

Not altogether. In the first place, this restriction applies only to material acquired on or after 1 August 1989. Secondly, there are special agreements with the production industries to allow lending facilities under agreed terms. It is best to check the conditions of purchase for particular materials in the library (see also the Section 10 on licences).

454 Why are public libraries excluded?

Because the Copyright Act stipulates that lending by public libraries of these materials is an infringement. Furthermore the regulations on lending and rental prohibit public libraries from lending material not covered by the Public Lending Right scheme.

455 Supposing there is no licensing scheme available?

The Secretary of State has the power to implement a scheme subject to appropriate payment as determined by the Copyright Tribunal if necessary.

456 What about the rights that performers have in sound recordings such as singers or instrumentalists?

If it is allowed to lend the sound recording then no rights of performers are infringed by that act of lending.

Publication right

457 How does publication right apply to sound recordings?

It is not applicable. There is no publication right for sound recordings.

Films and videos

Definition

458 What is the definition of a film?

The definition of a film includes anything from which a moving image can be produced. This covers video, videodisk, optical disc and any other new technologies which produce moving images. Despite its name a microfilm is not a film but a photograph!

Authorship

459 Who is the author of a film?

The producer and the principal director. Note that it is presumed that all films have both producers and principal directors and therefore all films are treated as having joint authorship unless these two functions are performed by the same person. Note that this applies only to films made on or after 1 July 1994. Before that date the author is defined simply as 'the person responsible for making the arrangements necessary for making the film'.

460   Do the authors of films enjoy moral rights?

Yes, the producer and principal director both enjoy moral rights in the same way as authors of literary works.

Ownership of copyright

461   Who owns the copyright in a film?

See Section 3 on Ownership for more detailed information. This will depend on the contracts between the various people who made the film. Remember that the film will have many copyright elements.

Example. A filmed interview with a song writer contains several performances of the songwriter's songs and an extract of a film containing performances of some of these songs. The songwriter may own the copyright in his or her words in the interview and in the words and music of the songs; the person making the TV programme will own the copyright in the programme as a whole; and the film maker will own some elements at least of the copyright in the extract of the film included in the programme.

462   Are the rules for extended and revived copyright the same?

Not quite. The extended copyright will be owned by the person who owned the copyright on 31 December 1995 but the revived copyright in the film will be owned by the principal director or his/her personal representative. But they will not own any revived copyright in the various elements of the film such as the screenplay and music, and will need to negotiate with the owners of the copyright of these elements, if they are still in copyright, for rights to exploit the revived copyright in the film as a whole.

Duration of copyright

463   Do the rules about works originating in the EEA (see paragraph 70ff) also apply?

Yes, the rules in this area are the same. To save repetition, the 70 year rule is marked with a * to remind you that the EEA/non-EEA rules apply.

464   How long does the copyright in a film last?

Copyright in film lasts for 70* years from the end of the year in which the last of the following died:

* the principal director
* the author of the screenplay
* the author of the dialogue
* the composer of music specially created for and used in the film.

provided at least one author is an EEA national or the film was first released in an EEA country. See paragraph 71 for other rules.

465   It is not always easy to find out who all these people are or when they died. What can be done then?

When the identity of at least one of them is known, then copyright expires as in paragraph 59.

466   What if the identity of none of them can be found?

Then copyright expires 70* years from the end of the year in which the film was made unless, during that time it was made available to the public.

467   What happens if it was made available to the public?

Then copyright runs for 70* years from the end of the year in which that took place.

468   Is 'made available to the public' the same as 'published'?

Not quite. In the context of a film it means being shown in public or included in a broadcast or cable television programme.

469 Sometimes nobody in particular is responsible for making a film. What happens about copyright then?

If it is not possible to say that anyone took on the distinctive responsibilities outlined in paragraph 464 then none of these rules apply and copyright expires 50 years from the end of the year in which the film was made.

470 Does the soundtrack of a film count as a sound recording or a film?

The soundtrack of a film counts as part of the film and therefore gets the length of protection of the film, not just as a sound recording.

Copying films

471 What rights does the copyright owner have?

The owner has the same rights as for literary, dramatic and musical works.

472 Does this include copying from one medium to another?

Yes. To make a copy of, say, a film to become a video is copying the work.

473 Supposing the medium on which the work is stored is obsolete? Can copies be made on to a usable type of equipment?

Not without the permission of the copyright owner.

Fair dealing

474 Is there fair dealing in films?

There is fair dealing in film or video only for the specific cases mentioned below.

475   Research or private study
There is no fair dealing in films or videos for research or private study.

476   Reporting current events
See paragraph 427.

477   Criticism and review
See paragraph 428.

Library and archive copying

478   Can libraries or archives copy films or videos in their collections?
In general, no. The special provisions for library and archive copying apply only to literary, dramatic or musical works but not to other works.

479   What is to be done for a researcher who needs a copy of part of a film or video?
The copy cannot be supplied unless the copyright in the material is owned by the library or archive or the original copyright owner has given permission for copies to be made.

480   Can they make copies for other archives?
Not under copyright law. They may have other agreements with production companies which allow this.

Educational copying

481   Can films be copied for classroom use?
No. But there is an exception for training in the making of films or film soundtracks and then only by the teacher or pupil themselves. But they can be played or viewed by the class as they are broadcast.

482 Copying as a condition of export
See paragraph 273.

483 Material open to public inspection
See paragraph 277.

484 Public administration
See paragraph 441.

Multimedia

485 If a publication contains material in several different forms such as a booklet, computer program and video, how is the copyright worked out?
The copyright will subsist separately in each item and the rules for each format will apply. So the copyright in the entire package could run out at several different times. In that sense, it is no different from a periodical issue. It may also be a database (see Section 9).

486 Who is the author of a mixed-media package?
The rules for ownership and authorship are the same as for each of the components. However, the publisher will almost certainly own copyright in the format of the whole package.

487 Issuing copies to the public
This is an exclusive right of the owner.

488 Performing the work
The owner has the exclusive right to perform the work. For other matters relating to performance of a work see paragraph 443ff, as the same basic rules apply and the same problems arise.

489 Broadcasting the work
See paragraph 448ff.

490 Adaptation

The owner has the exclusive right to adapt the work.

Lending and rental

491 If this right is an exclusive right of the owner, does this mean that lending services for video materials are not allowed?

No. Lending by prescribed libraries (other than public libraries) is allowed provided that any charges made cover no more than the administrative costs of making the loan.

492 Does this mean that public libraries may no longer lend videos?

Not altogether. In the first place, this restriction applies only to material acquired on or after 1 August 1989. Secondly, there may well be special agreements with the production industries to allow rental/lending facilities under agreed terms. It is best to check either the conditions of purchase for particular materials in the library or seek advice on the latest situation from The Library Association (see appendix of useful addresses).

493 Why are public libraries excluded?

Because public libraries may lend only materials which (a) were purchased before December 1996 or (b) are covered by the Public Lending Right scheme or (c) are covered by special agreements with the industry at large or with specific production companies or their agents.

494 Supposing there is no lending scheme available?

The Secretary of State has the power to implement a scheme subject to appropriate payment as determined by the Copyright Tribunal if necessary.

495   What about the rights that performers such as singers or instrumentalists have in films and videos?

If it is allowed to lend the film or video then no rights of performers are infringed by that act of lending.

Publication right

496   Are films subject to publication right?

Yes, in the same way as literary, dramatic and musical works (see paragraph 326ff).

Broadcasts

Most matters relating to broadcasts, from a library and archive point of view, are dealt with under either 'sound recordings' or 'films'. However, the section on databases should also be consulted.

Definition

497 What is the definition of a broadcast?

The definition of a broadcast is a transmission by wireless telegraphy of visual images, sounds or other information which is capable of being lawfully received by the public.

498 So is a cable programme service different?

Yes, a cable programme service is defined as a service which consists of sending visual images, sounds or other information by means of a telecommunications system (but not by wireless telegraph) for reception at two or more places (whether at the same time or not) in response to requests by different users.

499 This all sounds rather technical. Does it really matter what the difference is?

Sometimes. Essentially a cable programme service is one that is viewed on demand and is not 'live'. This can be important when discussing the legal status of websites.

Authorship

500 Who is the author of a broadcast?

Essentially it is the person who transmits the programme if that person has any responsibility for its contents.

501 Does the author enjoy moral rights?

Once again, in a word, no!

Ownership of copyright

502 Who owns the copyright in a broadcast?

Usually the person who transmits the programme.

503 What about a broadcast which includes a record?

There are separate copyrights in the broadcast and the sound recording included in it. In the same way a television programme which includes a film has separate copyrights in the television transmission and the film in the programme.

504 As broadcasts often come from many different countries, which one is regarded as the original?

The country where the uninterrupted signal started is regarded as the country of origin.

505 Supposing it is a satellite broadcast?

New legislation makes it clear that, where the satellite is merely a retransmission point, it has no significance in determining where the broadcast came from.

Duration of copyright

506   When does the copyright in a broadcast expire?

Copyright in a broadcast expires 50 years after the year when the broadcast was made or the programme was included in a cable television service.

507   What about repeats?

The fact that a programme was repeated does not extend or renew the copyright.

Copying

Fair dealing

508   Is there fair dealing in broadcasts?

Fair dealing in broadcasts is allowed for reporting current events and for criticism and review but it is not allowed for cable programme services (because they are never 'live' and therefore are not current in the same way as broadcasts).

509   Supposing I want to record something because I am out and will miss it or it clashes with another programme I want to watch/hear?

Copying from the radio or television for personal use to listen or view at a more convenient time is allowed provided that the copy is used only for private purposes. This is technically called 'time-shifting'.

510   Supposing I ask friends round to watch the recording?

Provided they were friends or relations and you did not make any charge this would be legal.

Educational copying

511 Can broadcasts be copied for classroom use, too?

Only with the appropriate licence and such licences are now generally available for education establishments. See Section 10. One exception is for training in the making of films or film soundtracks and then only by the teacher or pupil themselves. But the films can be played or viewed by the class as they are broadcast.

Library and archive copying

512 Can libraries and archives record off-air for their collections?

This is permitted only for specified collections, which at the time of writing are: British Film Institute, British Library, British Medical Association, British Music Information Centre, Imperial War Museum, Music Performance Research Centre, National Library of Wales, and the Scottish Film Council.

513 Can archives keep off-air recordings made for 'time-shifting' purposes?

No. They must be kept and used by the person who made them for their own use. Only designated archives can retain material for archival purposes. Copies made under the ERA licence are a different matter and can be kept indefinitely.

514 Supposing someone's papers are deposited with an archive and these papers include copies of audiovisual materials such as off-air recordings, can the archive keep these?

In theory, no. They are infringing copies because off-air recording can be done only for certain limited purposes and storing the copies in an archive is not one of them.

515 Lending and rental

This is not relevant to broadcasts or cable television pro-grammes. Copies of broadcasts which may be lent or rented will be considered as sound recordings or films.

516 Publication right

This is not relevant to broadcasts and cable television pro-grammes.

Databases and electronic materials

517 It is very important to distinguish between electronic material and databases. One is the format in which a work is stored or transmitted, the other is a form of a work itself. There are many works which are electronic but are not databases and equally many databases that are not electronic! This chapter tries to deal with some of these questions, but users of this book should realize that this is a constantly-changing situation and the subject-matter, questions and answers are all moving targets. Because the term 'electronic materials' can cover works in electronic form, computer programs and databases these items will be dealt with separately within the usual headings in this chapter although they are all linked together in some respects.

518 There are many copyright questions which arise in the electronic world to which the answers are exactly the same as in the more traditional paper-based world. However, some issues are peculiar to electronic materials and some of the answers which are quite clear in the paper world are not so obvious when we deal with electronic materials. The introduction of new legislation on databases makes many of they answers different if the work is considered a database.

Databases

Definitions

519   Are databases protected by copyright?

Databases can certainly be subject to copyright but they are now also subject to a quite separate Database Right.

520   What is the definition of a database?

A database is defined as: 'a collection of works, data or other materials which:

- are arranged in a systematic or methodical way, and
- are individually accessible by electronic or other means'.

521   Can a literary work also be a database?

Yes, it can. In order to be recognized as a literary work, a database will be eligible only if it is original (a vital test for copyright protection) and the selection or the contents and arrangement of the database constitutes the author's own intellectual creation. In this case the database will acquire both copyright and Database Right protection.

522   Must a database be electronic to be protected?

Definitely not. The phrase 'other means' makes it quite clear.

Copyright and Database Right

523   A database can be subject to both copyright and Database Right and it is very important to remember this when reading the following paragraphs.

524   What is the difference between copyright and Database Right?

Essentially a database is subject to copyright if it is a work of personal intellectual activity; otherwise it does not attract copyright but does attract the new Database Right.

525   Are all databases now protected by Database Right?

Not necessarily. To qualify for Database Right the contents of the database must have been assembled as the result of substantial investment in obtaining, verifying or presenting the contents.

526   Does investment just mean money?

No. Investment specifically includes financial, human or technical resources.

527   If the database is made up of material which is not copyright, is the database still protected?

Yes, if it qualifies as a database. The copyright status of the content of a database is irrelevant. It is the construction of the database that is the key question.

The following table might help to clarify this rather complex situation.

Content	Arrangement	Select, verify, present	Protection © = copyright; DR = Database Right; X = no protection	Example
Copyright	Original	Yes	© DR	*Chemical Abstracts*
Copyright	Not original	Yes	© X DR	*Books in Print*
Copyright	Original	No*	©© X	Existing collection of recent papers rearranged by subject
Copyright	Not original	No	© X X	Collection of author's own papers by date

continued overleaf

Not copyright	Original	Yes	X © DR	Selected C18 sermons by subject
Not copyright	Not original	Yes	XXDR	Telephone white pages
Not copyright	Original	No*	X © X	Existing collection of C18 papers rearranged by subject
Not copyright	Not original	No	XXX	Tough!

*It seems unlikely that this situation could happen as arrangement or re-arrangement would probably result in a different form of presentation.

Authorship

528   Who is the author of a database?

Databases rarely have personal authors. For this reason the law recognizes authors in specific circumstances only, otherwise they are designated 'makers'. But if personal authorship can be demonstrated (as in a scholarly bibliography for example) then the person creating the database is the author and the usual rules of authorship apply. If no author can be demonstrated databases are considered anonymous and only Database Right protection can be claimed. The maker of a database is the person who takes the initiative in obtaining, verifying or presenting the contents of the database and assumes the risk of investing in those actions and therefore obtains the Database Right. Makers cannot qualify for this right unless they are individuals with EEA nationality or companies/organizations incorporated within the EEA or part-nerships or unincorporated bodies formed under the law of an EEA state.

Ownership of copyright and Database Right

529 Where copyright subsists, the copyright rules apply (see Section 3). Ownership of Database Right is the maker of the database, although the usual rules about ownership of works made as part of employment or for the Crown apply.

Duration of copyright and Database Right

530 When a database attracts copyright protection the usual rules of duration of copyright for literary works apply (see paragraph 67ff). When Database Right applies this lasts for 15 years from the end of the year in which the database was completed. If, during that time, it is made available to the public, then the 15 year term runs from the end of the year in which the database was made available.

531 **But databases are constantly being updated. What happens to the length of protection then?**

If substantial changes, including accumulation of data, additions or deletions take place so that the new database would be considered the subject of substantial new investment, then the 15 year period will begin again. In other words, where a database is frequently being updated it will remain protected by Database Right for 15 years after the final changes have been made.

532 **What about old databases?**

Where a database was completed after 1 January 1983 and the Database Right began to operate when the regulations came into force, then that database obtains Database Right until 31 December 2013.

533 **What about databases which already exist but which would not qualify for copyright under the new rules?**

If the database was made before 27 March 1996 and was copyright immediately before the regulations come into force, then it remains in copyright under the usual rules for copyright duration.

Owner's rights

534 The rights that owners have in the copyright of a database are much the same as those for literary, dramatic and musical works (see paragraph 40ff). The rights of Database Rights owners are defined in a different way.

535 What rights does the owner of Database Right have?
The owner of the Database Right has the right to prevent the extraction or re-utilization of all or a substantial part of the contents of the database.

536 What precisely does 'extraction' mean?
The word 'extraction' is defined as 'permanent or temporary transfer of the contents to another medium by any means or in any form'.

537 Does this mean that nothing can ever be taken from a database?
No. A user is allowed to extract small amounts of data provided that the amount taken is insubstantial.

538 What counts as 'insubstantial'?
This is not defined but in deciding if the amount taken is substantial or not quality and quantity are both factors, separately and together. So it is possible to take a small quantity but still infringe the Database Right because of the quality of what has been taken. The reverse is also true.

For example, it might be considered that three or four entries from different parts of the 'white' telephone pages is not substantial but to take the addresses of all four companies listed in the *Yellow Pages* under a highly specific classification could be substantial.

539 Supposing someone copies an insubstantial amount one day and then does the same a few days later. Is this allowed?

No. The law has spotted this cunning ploy. It specifies that systematic extraction of insubstantial parts of a database may amount to extraction of substantial amounts. In other words, extractions done at different times must be seen as cumulative.

540 What about 're-utilization'? Does this stop me using any information?

No. 'Re-utilization' is defined as 'making the contents available to the public by any means'. Re-utilization is dealt with under 'Fair dealing'.

541 Surely this is making facts subject to copyright?

Not really. Copyright and the other rights associated with it refer to using someone else's property. Imagine someone has compiled a list of ice-cream makers in East Coast resorts. There is nothing to stop someone else compiling their own list and issuing this as a free or commercial product provided they have compiled it from scratch and not used the other person's list. The idea behind Database Right is to give some protection to the person who invested in putting the data together in the first place, not to give them exclusive control over those facts but the way those facts have been assembled and made available.

Fair dealing

542 Are databases subject to fair dealing in the same way as literary works?

Yes, but with an important difference. Where a database is *copyright* then it is subject to fair dealing for research or private study provided the source is indicated. Where the database is subject only to Database Right then the following rules apply.

543   Does this mean that if I find some information I can at least use it?

Yes, on two counts. Firstly, if you need to use a substantial part of the database, you can do this provided that it is for non-commercial research or private study. So you can certainly look up the addresses of the five or six ice-cream manufacturers in Bridlington and Scarborough and write them down for your own use but this information cannot be issued to the public in the form of a trade directory, database or in any other way. It seems highly unlikely that you would need to write down on your piece of paper by the telephone the source of the information to comply with this rule! Secondly, if the amount taken is insubstantial and you are a lawful user of the database you can extract *and* re-utilize this information, in other words use it and re-package it for publication or further use. But remember that insubstantial amounts will be very small amounts indeed!

544   Why is commercial research excluded?

The law is quite specific that *anything* done to a database for the purposes of research for a commercial purpose is not fair dealing with that database.

545   What constitutes a lawful user?

A lawful user is someone who has a right to use the database. In a paper context this is anyone entitled to use the library where it is stored or any private owner of a database or anyone they permit to have access to it. In the electronic context it will be anyone who legitimately has a licence to use or be allowed to use the database.

546   Are users of library services lawful users?

This will depend on the licence the library has with the database owner. In electronic situations it is important to ensure that the library's licence includes as wide a range of users as possible so that nobody is excluded. For commercial companies lawful users may be a much more restricted group (i.e. company employees only or even only those in the R&D department).

547   Some electronic databases come with very strict licences. Can these prevent any use of the database at all?

Not legally. The terms of any contract which aims to prevent a lawful user from extracting or re-utilizing insubstantial parts of the database will be considered null and void in law.

Educational copying

548   Can databases be copied for educational purposes?

Where a database is protected only by copyright then the usual rules apply. Where Database Right exists then this is not infringed if a substantial part is extracted for the purposes of illustration for teaching or research and this is not done for any commercial purpose and the source is acknowledged.

549   Does this mean to illustrate research?

This is not at all clear. Whether 'illustration' belongs with teaching or 'teaching and research' is not stated. The words given are those from the law – only a judge may ever sort this out!

Library and archive copying

550   Can databases be made available through libraries?

Essentially the answer is 'yes'. Certainly under a licence from the database owner this can be done but it is essential to ensure that all legitimate users of the library are designated as 'lawful users', otherwise they do not have the right to use any of the material in the database. If the database is in paper format, problems of access do not arise in copyright terms but the issue of what users may copy will remain.

551   Can libraries copy parts of databases for users?

Where a database is copyright (only) then libraries may copy them as they can other literary works (a reasonable proportion); however, library copying is not permitted for Database Right so the abilities of libraries to copy in this respect are limited to copying an insubstantial part.

Adaptation

552   Supposing someone took a database, altered the way it was arranged and then re-issued it.

This is not allowed as the law specifically defines adaptation as including arrangement or alteration of the version or translation.

Lending and Rental

553   Presumably libraries cannot lend databases?

Yes, they can. It is easy to think that database = electronic database but these rules apply to paper copies too. So, the lending of a database as defined by paragraph 310 is not considered as extraction or re-utilization and is therefore allowed under the same conditions as literary works. Similarly, on-the-spot reference is permitted. See paragraph 310ff for lending and rental.

Making copies available for public inspection

554   Can databases be made available for public inspection?

Similar rules to those for literary works apply to databases.

Public administration

555   Similar rules to those for literary works apply to databases.

Computer programs

556 Are computer programs a separate sort of work?

In some ways but not in others. Although computer programs are classed as literary works, some special conditions apply.

557 What about computer programs that have been printed out?

These are literary works. See paragraph 43ff.

558 A lot of work goes into preparing the design of a computer program. Is that protected as well?

It would in any case be considered as a literary work but the law does specify this type of work as being protected.

559 Who is the author of a computer program?

The person who wrote the program.

560 How long does copyright in a computer program last?

The same as a literary work (see paragraph 67ff).

561 Are computer programs subject to fair dealing?

Yes, but just how this could work in practice is difficult to determine. One area where a sort of 'fair dealing' exists is to allow the translation of a lower language program into a higher language. Strangely the law excludes this activity under fair dealing but specifically allows it in another part of the legislation! This must be done by a lawful user of the program.

562 What about making back-up copies?

If a lawful user needs to make a back-up copy for lawful use of the program then this is not an infringement of copyright. 'Lawful use' is not defined.

563 Supposing a programmer wants to use the program to create a quite separate program? Can the program be decompiled for this purpose?

Yes, provided that the necessary conditions are met. These are that the information obtained through decompiling the program is not used for any other purpose than creating an independent program which must not be similar to the one decompiled. In addition the information must not be passed on to anyone unless they need to know for the purposes of creating the new program, nor must the information be readily available through any other source.

564 Sometimes contracts forbid some of the copying outlined in the previous paragraphs. Can anything be done?

Yes, the law specifically states that where a contract tries to prevent any of these actions then that element of the contract is null and void.

Educational copying

565 Can computer programs be copied for educational purposes?

Only with the consent of the copyright owner directly or under licence. Some software is made available specifically for educational purposes and is free of copyright restrictions provided it is not exploited for commercial purposes.

Library and archive copying

566 Can computer programs be copied by libraries and archives for their users?

No, unless it is possible to determine what is a reasonable proportion of a computer program and it could then be copied for the reader as part of a non-periodical work (see paragraph 179ff). In practice the answer is simply 'no'.

567 What happens if the library has a computer program or other electronic material which becomes unusable for technical reasons? Can it be copied so that it can continue to be used?

Yes, provided that the conditions of purchase do not prohibit such copying and the original copy must not be retained, otherwise it becomes an infringing copy.

Broadcasting

568 This is not really applicable to computer programs. Where a work is in electronic format the same rules apply as if it were in paper format.

Lending and rental

569 Can computer programs be lent or rented out?

They can be lent, other than by public libraries, but cannot be rented without the copyright owner's consent.

Other electronic materials

570 Are electronic materials defined in legal terms?

Yes. 'Electronic' means actuated by electric, magnetic, electromagnetic, electro-chemical or electromechanical energy, and 'in electronic form' means in a form usable only by electronic means.

571 So are electronic materials a separate group of protected works?

No. What is protected is the content of the electronic material and the electronic version of it. This is just like a paper copy where the contents of a book are protected but so is the typography.

572   But electronic materials always need some software to make them work. Is this part of the copyright in the work?

No. It is important to distinguish between the content of the work and the supporting computer systems. The latter will be copyright in their own right as computer software. It would be possible, for example, to have an electronic document which was out of copyright but software which was certainly still protected.

573   Who is the author of an electronic work?

The author of the content of an electronic work will be decided in the same way as if that work were not electronic. In other words if it is an electronic text, think of it as a book or periodical article, if it is a picture, consider whether it is a photograph or painting and so on.

574   If the work is scanned or digitized who will be the author of the electronic version?

It is unlikely that the scanned or digitized version of a work will have an individual author. Unless one can specifically be identified the electronic version will be considered anonymous and the rules for anonymous works will apply.

575   Does authorship really matter in electronic documents?

Yes, and it will become a vital issue. Researchers and users generally want to know who was responsible for a document, database or any other work as this has a bearing on its importance and value. It also gives an idea of the point of view behind an author's work. It is also possible now to use technology to link authorship to payment. Anyway, those who write really do want the credit, even if there is no money involved.

576   Do authors of electronic materials enjoy moral rights?

Yes, and they are very important in an electronic context. It is very easy to change content or authorship, or conceal the origin of a work in an electronic context and all of these are moral rights enjoyed by authors. Essentially the same rules apply as for the paper world.

Duration

577   How long does copyright in an electronic work last?

So far as the content is concerned, the same rules apply as if the work were not electronic.

578   But if a new edition of a work causes a new term of copyright, what constitutes a new edition of an electronically stored work?

That is difficult to decide. Obviously if a whole new piece is added then the work is a new edition but if, as in the case of a database, material is added frequently, and in small pieces, it is difficult to say whether every addition creates a new edition or whether a lot of new data has to be added before this can be claimed. A further problem is that no actual printed version will be made every time a change is made so some editions may come and go and never be known about. Special rules apply to databases.

Copying

Fair dealing

579   Is there fair dealing in electronic works?

This is not an easy question to answer. Technically there is fair dealing in the content of any electronic work where that content qualifies for fair dealing as a literary, dramatic, musical or artistic work. However, as electronic works can be accessed usually only by the use of passwords and a contract with the supplier, what can and cannot be done by a user is governed more by the terms of that contract and the issue of the password, rather than by copyright law as such. A further consideration is what is 'fair' in electronic terms. Fair dealing is not limited to copying but this is the most usual form which it takes. But the idea of 'fair' (see paragraph 115ff) may be difficult to justify in an electronic world when it is so easy to exactly reproduce a work, store and retransmit it and even change it. Whether fair dealing generally exists in an electronic world has never been tested. It should but it may or may not, depending on the circumstances. The World Intellectual Property Organisation (WIPO) – the body responsible for administering international copyright treaties – has supported the idea that fair dealing should exist in the electronic environment.

580   Is copying from teletext such as Oracle or Ceefax allowed?

According to the law, no. Such information services are cable television programmes and, as such, are not available for fair dealing purposes. However, the producers often permit copying by means of printers connected to the television receiver and this is then a licence, actual or implied, from the copyright owner. The conditions of any such licence must be complied with and material copied must not be used for commercial republication or other unfair purposes.

Issue of copies to the public

581   This is an exclusive right of the copyright owner and needs to be interpreted in both the context of online activity and physical carriers such as CD-ROMs or DVDs.

Performance

582   Are the rights of performance relevant to electronic materials?

Yes, in two respects. Firstly the content of an electronic document may be multimedia in nature with songs, speeches or dancing. These all have rights of performance in them. Secondly, allowing an electronic work to be viewed in public by a number of people can also be considered performance and an infringement.

Lending and Rental

583   Can electronic materials be rented?

Rental, as for all other copyright works, is an exclusive right of the copyright owner and this includes both works in electronic form and computer programs as such.

584   What about lending electronic materials?

From a legal point of view, both computer programs and works in electronic form can be lent. In practice, these products are usually sold with restrictions included in the contract so that they cannot be lent or used on premises other than those specified in the contract. If there is no specific contract then it should be possible to lend, for example, a CD-ROM within the limits for lending specified in paragraph 310ff.

585   Supposing a library has a work in electronic form and another library wants to consult it. Can the second library be given access for a limited time?

Probably not. The contract giving access will define who can use a particular electronic work.

586   Is it meaningful to talk about lending in an electronic sense?

Yes, for two reasons. Firstly, electronic materials may still be on physical carriers, such as disks, and these could be physically lent. Secondly, lending really results in passing something to someone else so that the owner of it does not have use of it for a limited time while the other person does. This can now be achieved electronically by transmitting something to someone and (*a*) putting a 'block' on access to it while it is being used elsewhere and (*b*) constructing automatic erasing mechanisms so that the 'borrowing' library or person loses the work after the specified time. Watch out for developments in this area.

Publication Right

587   Are electronic materials generally subject to Publication Right?

Theoretically, yes but where do you find such materials out of copyright!!?

Computer-generated works

588   Some works are generated automatically by computer, so who is the author of a computer-generated work?

The law says it is the person by whom the arrangements necessary for the creation of the work were undertaken.

589   Is it really possible for a work to be totally computer-generated?

This is open to debate. Although there are documents which can be generated automatically, somewhere along the line a human person set up the program to generate the work or at least gave the computer some instructions on how this should be done subsequently.

590   How long does the copyright in a computer-generated work last?

The copyright in a computer-generated work expires 70 years from the end of the year in which the work was made.

Websites

591 Websites present all kinds of copyright problems

The paragraphs below give some indication of the problems
libraries may face when considering using website technology to
develop their services. You will need to consider who owns the
website and whether the website constitutes a database as
defined in law. Other issues include the status of a website
(whether a broadcast or a cable programme service) and liability
of website providers.

**592 Is it an infringement to put works on the internet or
world wide web?**

Yes. Mounting text or images on the WWW is a form of issuing
copies to the public and must be seen in the same way as any
other form of distribution.

**593 But supposing a document is put on the WWW but
nobody ever downloads it. Is this still an infringement?**

Yes, because the document has been issued to the public in that
it is widely available to the public for reading, viewing or copying
if they wish. The fact that nobody does copy the work is another
matter. It is an infringement of copyright to issue copies of a
work to the public, even if this is done without charge, unless the
person issuing the copies has the right to do so. The fact that
nobody ever reads these copies is irrelevant!

**594 Does the fact that it is so easy to build links to other
websites pose any problems?**

Yes. If you build a link to another website it is best (*a*) to obtain
the permission of the website owner and (*b*) to make sure the
link is to the homepage and not into the body of the website
text. But it also depends on whether you build your link to the
homepage of the other website; build deep links (direct into the
text of the other website); use framed links (icons to click on

round the edge of the screen which obscure who actually owns the website); or embedded links (where an actual image from another website is embedded in your own to make the link direct).

595   Why go to so much trouble?

Because (*a*) the website owner may not wish his website to be associated with yours. You may be promoting views with which they strongly disagree; (*b*) you may bypass important information about ownership, conditions of use and even advertising, all of which the user would have found on the homepage; (*c*) if the user does not perceive that the information is owned by and made available though a different website provider from the one where the reader began the search, the reader may think the material is owned or supplied by the original website to which they logged on. This can cause the library to be accused of 'passing-off' – making services available which users think come from the library when, in fact, they belong to someone else.

596   Some websites have an icon to click for copyright information. Is this legal or necessary?

It is very necessary to ensure that users know exactly who owns what and what the user can do with material located. The icon prevents the user claiming ignorance of either ownership or conditions. Where websites start with a statement such as 'By clicking on this icon you agree that you have read the conditions of use and copyright statement' then the user is bound by those conditions and cannot plead ignorance.

597   Is all material on the web copyright?

Probably. To be safe, behave with material on the web as if it were in paper form. If you would not copy or distribute it in paper form, then do not do it in electronic form. That is, unless the owner specifically states this can be done – which many website owners do.

598   What about older text such as medieval manuscripts which have been put on the web by major libraries or archives?

The original text may be out of copyright but the electronic version will almost certainly attract its own copyright as it will have been created as a result of extensive research, editing and correction. Electronic images are rarely in a sufficiently good state to be mounted without careful attention. This may mean that a new copyright work has been created (but see paragraph 338). In addition, most websites probably qualify for protection as databases! Most certainly meet the criteria for this. So extraction and re-utilization of substantial parts would be excluded. Some experts also claim that a website may be either a broadcast or a cable programme service, so it is clear that the status of websites is anything but clear.

Licensing schemes

599 What is a licensing scheme?

Basically it is a scheme which allows someone who is not the copyright owner to use copyright material beyond the limits of the law with the permission of the copyright owner.

600 Who administers such schemes?

They are administered by different organizations and these can change. They are briefly described in the following paragraphs.

601 What is the difference between a licensing scheme and a licence?

A licensing scheme is one which covers a defined range of works and is offered to a particular class of organization (e.g. government departments, academic institutions) and which anyone who is in the class named can join. So a scheme for universities must be open to any university to join it. Licences are user-specific.

602   Are licensing schemes relevant to libraries?

Certainly, because any licence held by the organization which owns or administers the library will almost certainly include copying done in the library. But it is unusual for licensing schemes to be only for the library. The library is part of a larger organization which is licensed as a whole.

603   Do libraries have to abide by the rules of such licences?

Yes. They represent a contract between the licensing agency and the licensee.

604   What are the details of such schemes?

Each scheme will vary according to the type of material covered and the type of organization holding the licence. The terms and conditions of licences vary from one type of organization to another and from one time to another, so anything said here about the terms of a licence should be checked with the licensing agency before a licence is considered. These notes are for general guidance only. Note too that a licence is a contract and that the terms of the contract are what count in the end, not advice or comments in a general book on copyright such as this one!

605   Many journals have details of payment to the Copyright Clearance Center in the USA printed on the bottom of the page. Must libraries pay these fees to CCC?

Payment should be made only if copying is done beyond what UK law permits. The Copyright Licensing Agency (CLA) currently acts as the agent for the CCC and they should be contacted in cases of doubt. The national copyright agencies work together to form an international network through which payments are transferred.

606   What about copying publications from other countries?

The CLA has agreements with a number of countries to collect royalties on behalf of copyright owners in those countries. An up-to-date list can be obtained from the CLA

607   What are the major licensing agencies and schemes?

The brief description below gives a general idea of each agency and the type of licence it offers. Specific details should be obtained from the appropriate agency.

608   Copyright Licensing Agency (CLA)

The Copyright Licensing Agency is the largest agency that libraries will encounter. It offers a range of licences to copy onto and from paper and can now offer licences for fax copying as well which is technically electronic copying. The CLA also has an agreement with the Design and Artists Copyright Society (DACS) so the CLA can now offer a licence which includes artistic works as well. The CLA licence allows you to assume that any work is licensed for copying unless (a) it comes from a country not listed by the CLA or (b) it is on the list of exclusions by type or specific work issued by the CLA from time to time. Licences usually stipulate the number of copies that can be made and how much of any one work can be copied. Here are some examples:

Educational copying. The licence allows one copy of one article from a periodical issue or 5% of a book or one chapter; one copy for each pupil in a class and one for the teacher, whether in school, college or university. Libraries may also be allowed to make one copy of such material for the short-loan collection, but the making of study packs under this licence is currently not allowed and is subject to a separate licence. LEA schools have a different method of computing what can be copied using a combination of the number of copies per pupil per authority combined with a pence-per-copy fee for additional copying. There is a separate licence for Independent Schools. The CLA licence for schools and universities also allows the making of a complete copy of a book or journal in large-print format for visually impaired students (and staff in the case of universities) provided that the work is not already commercially available in large print; copies must be in a type size of at least 16 point and only sufficient copies can be made for the number of students who require them. A more general licence for copying for visually impaired people is being prepared (Spring 2001).

Government departments. Licences are structured according the needs of the department but typically allow 9 nine copies of a periodical article or 5% or a chapter of a book or the whole of one case from law reports. Up to 19 copies may be licensed for designated committees.

Industry and commerce. A model licence was negotiated with the Confederation of British Industries (CBI) which they could recommend to their members (but could not negotiate for them). This is essentially a matrix consisting of the sector in which the company operates and the number of research staff they employ. Usually up to nine copies of one periodical article or one chapter from a book are allowed for internal purposes. A similar licence has been negotiated for legal firms with the Law Society.

The CLA also offers an *ad hoc* clearance service for copying beyond the limits of the licence held. Only available to licence holders, it is called CLARCS (CLA Rapid Clearance Service). This allows CLA licensees to quickly obtain permission to copy amounts which exceed the limits of their basic licence. The fees are set by the copyright holder for each work and clearance is available by telephone, fax or e-mail. The fee is charged to the licensee's account.

609   Christian Copyright Licensing International (CCLI)

CCLI offers a licence for the copying of both the words and music of many hymns. Licences are available for churches, schools and conference centres but the original work must be owned by the licensor. Borrowing copies from a library outside the licensed organization and then copying is not covered by the licence. The scheme is remarkable as the first to license copying of music of any kind.

610 Newspaper Licensing Agency (NLA)

The NLA offers two types of licence. Type A covers in-house clipping services and *ad hoc* copying. All copying is reported to the NLA on a transactional basis. The annual fee is determined by the number of copies made, the number of employees and the annual turnover; Type B is related only to the number of copies but has a minimum fee. Like that of the CLA the NLA licence is for paper copying only, although some electronic copying may be permitted soon.

611 Design & Artists Copyright Society

The licence here is slightly different from others in that it legitimizes existing infringing collections of slides in educational establishments as well as licensing the making of new slides. Organizations who join declare their infringing collections and pay a one-off fee for these; there is then an annual licence fee based on the number of slides made. The scheme includes all artistic works, including those published in books, and DACS offers an indemnity in the case of users being challenged. DACS also has an arrangement for licensing artistic works through the CLA licensing system.

612 Educational Recording Agency

The ERA offers a licence for educational establishments only for off-air recording of all terrestrial broadcasting. As there is no licence for cable or satellite broadcasting at present, these programmes may be freely recorded for educational purposes only. Once recorded a copy may be used for teaching and further copied within the terms of the licence. It may be kept in the library of the institution for which it was recorded and may be lent to others with an ERA licence. Recording does not have to be done on the premises – it could be done by a teacher or lecturer at home for subsequent use within the licensed premises.

613 Open University Educational Enterprises

The OUEE licence is clearly specific for OU output. Again it is available only to educational establishments. Payment is according to the number of recordings kept for more than 30 days. Recordings kept for less than 30 days are not paid for but all recordings must be registered.

614 HMSO

Recent changes in government policy mean that many documents published, or controlled, by HMSO may now be freely copied. Most legislation and similar material, many official reports and documents can all be copied and re-used. Single and multiple copies are allowed and documents may be included in other works (such as textbooks) and in websites and other publications. The Royal Coat of Arms may not be included as this has become a sort of Trademark or Guarantee of integrity. As this is a rapidly changing area, it is best to consult the HSMO website for the latest guidance. See **www.hmso.gov.uk/guides.htm**.

615 Ordnance Survey (OS)

Because maps are artistic works, copying of these by libraries is not permitted, although individuals may claim fair dealing. The OS has introduced a wide range of licences for education, local authorities, commercial and business, legal procedures and planning permissions. They are very detailed and liable to quite radical change from time to time, and it would be misleading to describe them all here. The most important one for the general public and public libraries is that OS allows a library to supply copies, or a member of the public to make copies, up to the following limits: four copies may be made provided they are from a single map and that no more than 625cm^2 (A4 size) is created and this is at the original size – no enlargements are allowed.

There are separate schemes for local authority and planning applications, and libraries are advised not to get involved in copying for these purposes as they may not be aware of the finer points of the agreement. Details of educational, commercial and other types of licence should be obtained from OS direct.

616   Goad Publishing

Goad, who publish many maps, have announced they will allow copying by libraries for bona fide students within the same limits as Ordnance Survey: 625cm^2 (A4) from one map. Proof of genuine student status is required.

617   British Standards Institution (BSI)

BSI issue special licences for classroom use. In the case of Standards in public collections, BSI has stated that it allows up to 10% of a standard to be copied without infringement.

618   British Library Document Supply Centre (BLDSC)

The British Library Document Supply Centre holds a licence from the CLA which allows it to make copies beyond the limits of the provisions for libraries in return for the payment of royalties set by the copyright owners. These royalties are collected in full from the requesting organization or person. Basically, when a copy is supplied through this service the following limitations do not apply:

* more than one copy of an item can be supplied
* more than one article from an issue of a periodical can be supplied
* signed declarations are not required
* non-prescribed libraries can behave as if they are prescribed libraries (adding material to stock, obtaining replacement material, etc.)
* fees to end-users need not be charged

- the purpose does not necessarily have to be research or private study.

Copies may not be further copied except under the strict terms of any CLA licence held by the organization receiving the copies.

619 British Phonographic Industries (BPI)

Public libraries may not lend sound recordings except under licence and such a licence has been negotiated by the LA with the BPI for public libraries (only). This is based on a combination of the number of copies of any one work held at any one service point and a 'holdback' period for new releases when they will not be lent. The agreement covers vinyl, CDs and cassettes but not other forms of digital recording. There is no licence fee. Currently, the Spoken Word Publishers Association (SWPA) are stepping outside this agreement and seeking a separate agreement in the light of the new legislation on lending and rental. Similarly, representatives of performers are also seeking compensation through a licensing scheme. Contact The Library Association for the latest position.

620 Performing Right Society (PRS)

PRS is one of the oldest licensing societies in the world. It licenses all public performances of music whether these are live or recorded, including public use of radios and television, on behalf of authors/composers.

621 Mechanical Copyright Protection Society (MCPS)

MCPS licenses the recording of music onto any medium and rerecording of music from abroad. Essentially MCPS licenses the making of a recording, while PRS licenses the public performance of that music and PLS licences the public use of the recording.

622   Phonographic Performance Ltd (PPL)

PPL is a music industry collecting society representing over 2500 record companies, from the large multinationals to the small independents. They collect licence fees from broadcast and *public* performance users on behalf of the record companies. This licence fee revenue, after deduction of running costs, is then distributed to record company members and to performers.

623   What about other licences?

There are an increasingly bewildering array of licences and permissions systems available. They include the JISC/PA guidelines and UK-wide HEFC licence; the NESLI (National Electronic Site Licence) and HERON (Higher Education on Demand). Also many individual publishers have their own tailor-made licences for different situations. It is impossible to do more than indicate that these exist and users should follow them up as necessary.

Other matters

International treaties

624 What importance does international copyright have?

Technically there is no such thing as 'international copyright'. Each country has its own copyright laws but most major countries belong to some or all of the three international conventions. Under these treaties and conventions each country protects the works produced in other countries as if they had been produced within its own borders, although usually works are not protected in a country for longer than they would be in the country of origin. So if a work is produced in a country where protection lasts for 50 years but is imported into a country where protection lasts for 70 years, then the work would still be protected for only 50 years in that country.

625 What are the three international conventions?

The Berne Copyright Convention, the Universal Copyright Convention (UCC) and the Trade-Related Intellectual Property

(TRIPS) element of the World Trade Agreement. A fourth, the WIPO Copyright Treaty, was agreed in 1996 but has not been ratified by enough countries to bring it into effect yet.

626   Are there any countries that do not belong to any of these conventions?

Yes, but the number is decreasing all the time. Those who have not signed one or more treaties cannot benefit from the liberalization of trade planned under the World Trade Agreement, so there is an incentive to reform or improve national copyright laws in most countries.

627   If a country does not belong to one of these treaties does this mean that their publications can be copied?

Perhaps. Although not all countries belong to one of the international treaties, one or two have signed bilateral agreements with the UK for mutual protection. It is best to check SI 1999/1751.

628   What is the importance of the copyright symbol? (©)

The idea of the © symbol is to indicate that the work was protected by copyright in the country of origin and had been registered for copyright protection. This is important under the Universal Copyright Convention, according to which publications without the symbol are not regarded as protected. As the USA has now joined the Berne convention, under which no formality is required for registering a copyright document, the symbol is chiefly important on publications from those countries which belong to the UCC but not to Berne. It also protects publications in those same UCC countries, so it is important for publishers to include it on their works even if it is not required in the country of origin as it should protect them when exported to UCC countries. Lack of the symbol in most countries has no significance.

Legal deposit

629 What is the connection between copyright deposit and copyright law?

None, nor has there been for many years. Copyright deposit is there to enable the designated libraries to build up collections of the national printed archive. However, there are proposals to extend legal deposit in the UK to non-print materials, including publications in electronic form such as CD-ROMs. At present, deposit of electronic materials, as well as sound recordings, depends on a voluntary code of practice agreed between the so-called copyright libraries and the publishing and record industries.

630 Why is it called copyright deposit?

Because it used to be a prerequisite for being able to claim copyright. But international conventions require that no formality is necessary before claiming copyright. Really copyright deposit should now be called 'legal deposit'.

Public Lending Right (PLR)

631 Is there a connection between PLR and copyright?

Yes. This was not true until the introduction of the Lending/Rental legislation but PLR and copyright are now firmly linked.

632 What is the connection between ISBNs, ISSNs and copyright?

Absolutely none. ISBNs, ISSNs and similar numbering systems are essentially tools of the bookselling and publishing industry which have been hijacked by librarians as useful systems for cataloguing, identifying and locating. Their presence or absence from a document has no bearing on its copyright status.

633 There has been a lot of talk about a right called 'droit de suite'. What is it?

Droit de suite is a right given to the creator of an original work of art (painting, sculpture, etc.) so that each time the work is sold the creator gets a percentage of the increased price, if there is one. This means that a painter who starts off as unknown and sells paintings for a few pounds can benefit from any subsequent fame achieved.

634 Does this have anything to do with libraries or archives?

Only if they have, or plan to acquire, collections of original works of art.

635 Has this right been introduced into the UK?

No, not yet. It was agreed by the European Parliament early in 1997 so it will take some time before it applies in the UK.

Other legislation

636 New human rights laws in the UK guarantee individuals the right of free speech. Can copyright be seen as infringing this human right?

No, because the assertion of the right of free speech cannot be used to take away private property from someone else. As copyright is a property law, this means you can express yourself any legal way you wish but not use someone else's property to do it.

637 How does copyright interact with Data Protection?

Although most data covered by the Data Protection Act will be liable to Database Rights, the rights conferred by the Data Protection Act do not change the rights of owners of databases at all.

638   What about Freedom of Information laws?

Again, rights of access to information do not change the rights
of owners of the copyright in that information.

List of useful addresses

Authors' Licensing & Collecting Society (ALCS)

Marlborough Court
14-18 Holborn
London EC1N 2LE
Tel: 020 7395 0600
Fax: 020 7395 0660
E-mail: alcs@alcs.co.uk
Website: **www.alcs.co.uk**

British Copyright Council

29–33 Berners Street
London W1P 4AA
Tel: 020 7306 4464
Fax: 020 7306 4740
E-mail: British.copyright.council@dial.pipex.com
Website: **www.britishcopyright.org.uk**

Copyright Licensing Agency

90 Tottenham Court Road
London W1P 9HE
Tel: 020 7436 5931
Fax: 020 7436 3986
E-mail: cla@cla.co.uk
Website: **www.cla.co.uk**

Design and Artists Copyright Society

Parchment House
13 Northburgh Street
London EC1V 0AH
Tel: 020 7336 8811
Fax: 020 7336 8822
Website: **www.dacs.co.uk**

Educational Recording Agency

Marlborough Court
14-18 Holborn
London EC1N 2LE
Tel: 020 7395 0600
Fax: 020 7395 0660
E-mail: alcs@alcs.co.uk
Website: **www.alcs.co.uk**

HMSO Copyright Section

St Clements
Colegate
Norwich NR3 1BQ
Tel: 01603 521000
Fax: 01603 723000
Website: (general) **www.hmso.gov/copy.htm**
　　　　　(guidelines) **www.hmso.gov.uk/guides.htm**

The Library Association
7 Ridgmount Street
London WC1E 7AE
Tel: 020 7255 0500
Fax: 020 7255 0501
E-mail: info@la-hq.org.uk
Website: **www.la-hq.org.uk**

Ministry of Defence
Hydrographic Department
Finance Section
Ministry of Defence
Taunton
Somerset TA1 2DN
Tel: 01823 337900

Newspaper Licensing Agency
Lonsdale Gate
Lonsdale Gardens
Tunbridge Wells
Kent TN1 1NL
Tel: 01892 525273
Fax: 01892 525275
E-mail: copy@nla.co.uk
Website: **www.nla.co.uk**

Ordnance Survey
Copyright Branch
Romsey Road
Maybush
Southampton SO9 4DH
Tel: 01703 792706
Fax: 01703 792535
Website: **www.ordsvy.gov.uk**

Performing Right Society

29/33 Berners Street
London W1P 4AA
Tel: 020 7306 4464
Fax: 020 7306 4740
Website: **www.prs.co.uk**

Public Lending Right Office

Richard House
Sorbonne Close
Stockton-on-Tees TS17 65DA
Tel: 01642 604699
Fax: 01642 615641
Website: **www.plr.com.uk**

Phonographic Performance Ltd

1 Upper James Street
London W1R 3HG
Tel: 0207 534 1000
Fax: 0207 534 1111
Website: **www.ppluk.com**

Selected further sources of information

Some useful books, journals and websites are listed below. The books must be viewed in the light of the dates on which they were published and will almost all need updating. The guides from The Library Association are particularly helpful.

Books

Norman, Sandy (ed.) (1999) *Copyright in further and higher education libraries*, 4th edn, ISBN 1 85604 322 3; *Copyright in health libraries* (1999), 3rd edn; ISBN 1 85604 323 1; *Copyright in industrial and commercial libraries* (1999), 4th edn; ISBN 1 85604 324 X; *Copyright in school libraries* (1999), 4th edn; ISBN 1 85604 326 6; *Copyright in public libraries* (1999), 4th edn, ISBN 1 85604 325 8; *Copyright in voluntary sector libraries* (1999), 3rd edn; ISBN 1 85604 327 4 (a series of six separate booklets which complements the information in this book). All published by Library Association Publishing.

Cornish, Graham P. (2000) *Understanding copyright in a week*, Hodder & Stoughton, ISBN 0 340 78241 2. A very general introduction for users, owners and creators.

Flint, Michael F. (1997) *A user's guide to copyright*, 4th edn, Butterworths, ISBN 0 406 04608 5.

Garnett, Kevin et al. (1999) *Copinger and Skone-James on copyright*, 14th edn, Sweet & Maxwell, 2 vols, ISBN 0 421 589 108. The Copyright Bible.

Henry, Michael (1998) *Current copyright law*, Butterworths. ISBN 0 406 896208. Gives the full text of the original Copyright Designs and Patents Act with all the amendments included in their correct place. This avoids the need to keep switching from one book to another.

Laddie, Hugh et al. (2000) *The modern law of copyright and designs*, 3rd edn, Butterworths, 3 vols, ISBN 0 406 910049

Merkin, Robert (1993, loose-leaf ongoing) *Copyright and design law*, Longman, ISBN 0 85121 797 4.

Pedley, Paul (2000) *Copyright for library and information services professionals*, 2nd edn, Aslib/IMI, ISBN 0 85142 432 5.

Phillips, Jeremy (1999) *Butterworths' intellectual property law handbook*, 4th edn, Butterworths, ISBN 0 40692 995 5.

Wall, Raymond A. (2000) *Copyright made easier*, 3rd edn, Aslib/IMI, ISBN 0 85142 447 3.

Periodicals

Aslib Guide to Copyright, Aslib, 1994. An ongoing loose-leaf publication.

Copyright Bulletin. Published quarterly by Unesco.

Copyright World. Published six times a year by Intellectual Property Publishing.

Industrial Property and Copyright. Monthly. Published by the World Intellectual Property Organization.

European Intellectual Property Review. Published monthly by ESC Publishing.

Websites

See also websites listed under 'Useful addresses'.

www.la-hq.org.uk/groups/laca/laca.html

The website for the Library Association Copyright Alliance which brings together most of the major players in the information provision industry to discuss copyright.

www.intellectual-property.gov.uk

A website maintained by the Patent Office to give information on a wide range of intellectual property issues. Copyright is well covered and there is a Frequently Asked Questions page.

www.wipo.org

To keep up with international developments in the World Intellectual Property Organization.

www.eblida.org

Useful for European developments, especially relating to libraries.

www.courtservice.gov.uk

Gives official transcripts of major cases. Searchable by subject.

www.bbc.co.uk/news

Surprisingly useful for latest news on copyright, especially in the media.

Extracts from the legislation

- SI 89/816 Copyright, Designs and Patents Act 1988
- SI 89/1212 The Copyright (Librarians and Archivists) (Copying of Copyright Material) Regulations 1989
- SI 96/2967 The Copyright and Related Rights Regulations 1996

Selected sections from the Copyright, Designs and Patents Act 1988 (SI 89/816)

General

29. (1) Fair dealing with a literary, dramatic, musical or artistic work for the purposes of research or private study does not infringe any copyright in the work or, in the case of a published edition, in the typographical arrangement.

(2) Fair dealing with the typographical arrangement of a published edition for the purposes mentioned in subsection (1) does not infringe any copyright in the arrangement.

(3) Copying by a person other than the researcher or student himself is not fair dealing if:

    (a)   in the case of a librarian, or a person acting on behalf of a librarian, he does anything which regulations under section 40 would not permit to be done under section 38 or 39 (articles or parts of published works: restriction on multiple copies of same material), or

    (b)   in any other case, the person doing the copying knows or has reason to believe that it will result in copies of substantially the same material being provided to more than one person at substantially the same time and for substantially the same purpose.

30. (1) Fair dealing with a work for the purpose of criticism or review, of that or another work or of a performance of a work, does not infringe any copyright in the work provided that it is accompanied by a sufficient acknowledgement

    (2) Fair dealing with a work (other than a photograph) for the purpose of reporting current events does not infringe any copyright in the work provided that (subject to subsection (3)) it is accompanied by a sufficient acknowledgement.

    (3) No acknowledgement is required in connection with the reporting of current events by means of a sound recording, film, broadcast or cable programme.

31. (4) The terms of a licence granted to an educational establishment authorising the reprographic copying for the purposes of instruction of passages from published literary, dramatic or musical works are of no effect so far as they purport to restrict the proportion of a work which may be copied (whether on payment or free of charge) to less than that which would be permitted under this section.

Libraries and archives

37. (1) In sections 38 to 43 (copying by librarians and archivists:

    (a)   references in any provision to a prescribed library or archive are to a library or archive of a description prescribed for the purposes of that provision by regulations made by the Secretary of State; and

(b) references in any provision to the prescribed conditions are to the conditions so prescribed.

(2) The regulations may provide that, where a librarian or archivist is required to be satisfied as to any matter before making or supplying a copy of a work:

(a) he may rely on a signed declaration as to that matter by the person requesting the copy, unless he is aware that it is false in a material particular, and

(b) in such cases as may be prescribed, he shall not make or supply a copy in the absence of a signed declaration in such form as may be prescribed.

(3) Where a person requesting a copy makes a declaration which is false in a material particular and is supplied with a copy which would have been an infringing copy if made by him:

(a) he is liable for infringement of copyright as if he had made the copy himself, and

(b) the copy shall be treated as an infringing copy.

(4) The regulations may make different provision for different descriptions of libraries or archives and for different purposes.

(5) Regulations shall be made by statutory instrument which shall be subject to annulment in pursuance of a resolution of either House of Parliament.

(6) References in this section, and in sections 38 to 43, to the librarian or archivist include a person acting on his behalf.

38. (1) The librarian of a prescribed library may, if the prescribed conditions are complied with, make and supply a copy of an article in a periodical without infringing any copyright in the text, in any illustrations accompanying the text or in the typographical arrangement.

(2) The prescribed conditions shall include the following:

(a) that copies are supplied only to persons satisfying the librarian that they require them for purposes of research or private study, and will not use them for any other purpose;

(b)   that no person is furnished with more than one copy of the same article or with copies of more than one article contained in the same issue of a periodical; and

(c)   that persons to whom copies are supplied are required to pay for them a sum not less than the cost (including a contribution to the general expenses of the library) attributable to their production.

39. (1)   The librarian of a prescribed library may, if the prescribed conditions are complied with, make and supply from a published edition a copy of part of a literary, dramatic or musical work (other than an article in a periodical) without infringing any copyright in the work, in any illustrations accompanying the work or in the typographical arrangement.

(2)   The prescribed conditions shall include the following:

(a)   that copies are supplied only to persons satisfying the librarian that they require them for purposes of research or private study, and will not use them for any other purpose;

(b)   that no person is furnished with more than one copy of the same material or with a copy of more than a reasonable proportion of any work; and

(c)   that persons to whom copies are supplied are required to pay for them a sum not less than the cost (including a contribution to the general expenses of the library) attributable to their production.

40. (1)   Regulations for the purposes of sections 38 and 39 (copying by librarian of article or part of published work) shall contain provision to the effect that a copy shall be supplied only to a person satisfying the librarian that his requirement is not related to any similar requirement of another person

(2)   The regulations may provide:

(a)   that requirements shall be regarded as similar if the requirements are for copies of substantially the same material at substantially the same time and for substantially the same purpose; and

      (b)   that requirements of persons shall be regarded as related if those persons receive instruction to which the material is relevant at the same time and place.

41. (1)   The librarian of a prescribed library may, if the prescribed conditions are complied with, make and supply to another prescribed library a copy of:

      (a)   an article in a periodical, or

      (b)   the whole or part of a published edition of a literary, dramatic or musical work,

without infringing any copyright in the text of the article or, as the case may be, in the work, in any illustrations accompanying it or in the typographical arrangement.

(2)   Subsection (1)(b) does not apply if at the time the copy is made the librarian making it knows, or could by reasonable inquiry ascertain, the name and address of a person entitled to authorise the making of the copy.

42. (1)   The librarian or archivist of a prescribed library or archive may, if the prescribed conditions are complied with, make a copy from any item in the permanent collection of the library or archive,

      (a)   in order to preserve or replace that item by placing the copy in its permanent collection in addition to or in place of it, or

      (b)   in order to replace in the permanent collection of another prescribed library or archive an item which has been lost, destroyed or damaged,

without infringing the copyright in any literary, dramatic or musical work, in any illustrations accompanying such a work or, in the case of a published edition, in the typographical arrangement.

(2)   The prescribed conditions shall include provision for restricting the making of copies to cases where it is not reasonably practicable to purchase a copy of the item in question to fulfil that purpose.

43. (1) The librarian or archivist of a prescribed library or archive may, if the prescribed conditions are complied with, make and supply a copy of the whole or part of a literary, dramatic or musical work from a document in the library or archive without infringing any copyright in the work or any illustrations accompanying it.

(2) This section does not apply if:

(a) the work had been published before the document was deposited in the library or archive, or

(b) the copyright owner has prohibited copying of the work,

and at the time the copy is made the librarian or archivist making it is, or ought to be, aware of that fact.

(3) The prescribed conditions shall include the following:

(a) that copies are supplied only to persons satisfying the librarian or archivist that they require them for purposes of research or private study and will not use them for any other purpose;

(b) that no person is furnished with more than one copy of the same material; and

(c) that persons to whom copies are supplied are required to pay for them a sum not less than the cost (including a contribution to the general expenses of the library or archive) attributable to their production.

75. (1) A recording of a broadcast or cable programme of a designated class, or a copy of such a recording, may be made for the purpose of being placed in an archive maintained by a designated body without thereby infringing any copyright in the broadcast or cable programme or in any work included in it.

(2) In subsection (1) "designated" means designated for the purposes of this section by order of the Secretary of State, who shall not designate a body unless he is satisfied that it is not established or conducted for profit.

Some definitions

175. (1) In this Part "publication", in relation to a work:

    (a) means the issue of copies to the public, and

    (b) includes, in the case of a literary, dramatic, musical or artistic work, making it available to the public by means of an electronic retrieval system;

and related expressions shall be construed accordingly.

  (2) In this Part "commercial publication", in relation to a literary, dramatic, musical or artistic work means:

    (a) issuing copies of the work to the public at a time when copies made in advance of the receipt of orders are generally available to the public, or

    (b) making the work available to the public by means of an electronic retrieval system;

and related expressions shall be construed accordingly.

  (4) The following do not contribute publication for the purposes of this Part and references to commercial publication shall be construed accordingly:

    (a) in the case of a literary, dramatic or musical work:

        (i) the performance of the work, or

        (ii) the broadcasting of the work or its inclusion in a cable programme service (otherwise than for the purposes of an electronic retrieval system);

    (b) in the case of an artistic work:

        (i) the exhibition of the work,

        (ii) the issue to the public of copies of a graphic work representing, or of photographs of, a work of architecture in the form of a building or a model for a building, a sculpture or a work of artistic craftsmanship,

        (iii) the issue to the public of copies of a film including the work, or

        (iv) the broadcasting of the work or its inclusion in a cable programme service (otherwise than for the purposes of an electronic retrieval system);

(c)   in the case of a sound recording or film:
    (i)   the work being played or shown in public, or
    (ii)   the broadcasting of the work or its inclusion in a cable programme service.

178. In this Part:

"article", in the context of an article in a periodical, includes an item of any description;

"computer-generated", in relation to a work, means that the work is generated by computer in circumstances such that there is no human author of the work;

"the Crown" includes the Crown in right of Her Majesty's Government in Northern Ireland or in any country outside the United Kingdom to which this Part extends;

"electronic" means actuated by electric, magnetic, electro-magnetic, electro-chemical or electro-mechanical energy, and "in electronic form" means in a form usable only by electronic means;

"reprographic copy" and "reprographic copying" refer to copying by means of a reprographic process;

"reprographic process" means a process:

(a)   for making facsimile copies, or

(b)   involving the use of an appliance for making multiple copies, and includes, in relation to a work held in electronic form, any copying by electronic means, but does not include the making of a film or sound recording.

SI 89/1212 The Copyright (Librarians and Archivists) (Copying of Copyright Material) Regulations 1989

Interpretation

2.   In these Regulations

"the archivist" means the archivist of a prescribed archive;

"librarian" means the librarian of a prescribed library;

"prescribed archive" means an archive of the descriptions specified in paragraph (4) of regulation 3 below;

"prescribed library" means a library of the descriptions specified in paragraphs (1), (2) and (3) of regulation 3 below.

Descriptions of libraries and archives

3.   (1)   The descriptions of libraries specified in Part A of Schedule 1 to these Regulations are prescribed for the purposes of section 38 and 39 of the Act:

Provided that any library conducted for profit shall not be a prescribed library for the purposes of those sections.

(2)   All libraries in the United Kingdom are prescribed for the purposes of sections 41, 42 and 43 of the Act as libraries the librarians of which may make and supply copies of any material to which those sections relate.

(3)   Any library of a description specified in Part A of Schedule 1 to these Regulations which is not conducted for profit and any library of the description specified in Part B of that Schedule which is not conducted for profit are prescribed for the purposes of sections 41 and 42 of the Act as libraries for which copies of any material to which those sections relate may be made and supplied by the librarian of a prescribed library.

(4)   All archives in the United Kingdom are prescribed for the purposes of sections 42 and 43 of the Act as archives which may make and supply copies of any material to which those sections relate and any archive within the United Kingdom which is not conducted for profit is prescribed for the pur-

poses of section 42 of the Act as an archive for which copies of any material to which that section relates may be made and supplied by the archivist of a prescribed archive.

(5)   In this regulation "conducted for profit", in relation to a library or archive, means a library or archive which is established or conducted for profit or which forms part of, or is administered by, a body established or conducted for profit.

Copying by librarian of article or part of published work

4.   (1)   For the purposes of sections 38 and 39 of the Act the conditions specified in paragraph (2) of this regulation are prescribed as the conditions which must be complied with when the librarian of a prescribed library makes and supplies a copy of any article in a periodical or, as the case may be, of a part of a literary, dramatic or musical work from a published edition to a person requiring the copy.

(2)   The prescribed conditions are:

(a)   that no copy of any article or any part of a work shall be supplied to the person the same unless:

(i)   he satisfies the librarian that he requires the copy for purposes of research or private study and will not use it for any other purpose; and

(ii)   he has delivered to the librarian a declaration in writing, in relation to that article or part of a work, substantially in accordance with Form A in Schedule 2 to these Regulations and signed in the manner therein indicated;

(b)   that the librarian is satisfied that the requirement of such person and that of any other person:

(i)   are not similar, that is to say, the requirements are not for copies of substantially the same article or part of a work at substantially the same time and for substantially the same purpose; and

(ii) are not related, that is to say, he and that person do not receive instruction to which the article or part of the work is relevant at the same time and place;

(c) that such person is not furnished:

(i) in the case of an article with more than one copy of the article or more than one article contained in the same issue of a periodical; or

(ii) in the case of a part of a published work, with more than one copy of the same material or with a copy of more than a reasonable proportion of any work; and

(d) that such person is required to pay for the copy a sum not less than the cost (including a contribution to the general expenses of the library) attributable to its production.

(3) Unless the librarian is aware that the signed declaration delivered to him pursuant to paragraph (2)(a)(ii) above is false in a material particular, he may rely on it as to the matter he is required to be satisfied on under paragraph (2)(a)(i) above before making or supplying the copy.

Copying by librarian to supply other libraries

5. (1) For the purposes of section 41 of the Act the conditions specified in paragraph (2) of this regulation are prescribed as the conditions which must be complied with when the librarian of a prescribed library makes and supplies to another prescribed library a copy of any article in a periodical or, as the case may be, of the whole or part of a published edition of a literary, dramatic or musical work required by that other prescribed library.

(2) The prescribed conditions are:

(a) that the other prescribed library is not furnished with more than one copy of the article or of the whole or part of the published edition; or

(b) that, where the requirement is for a copy of more than one article in the same issue of a periodical, or for a copy of the whole or part of a published edition, the other prescribed library furnishes a written statement to the effect that it is a prescribed library and that it does not know, and could not by reasonable inquiry ascertain, the name and address of a person entitled to authorise the making of the copy; and

(c) that the other prescribed library shall be required to pay for the copy a sum not less than the cost (including a contribution to the general expenses of the library) attributable to its production.

Copying by librarian or archivist for the purposes of replacing items in a permanent collection

6. (1) For the purposes of section 42 of the Act the conditions specified in paragraph (2) of this regulation are prescribed as the conditions which must be complied with before the librarian or, as the case may be, the archivist makes a copy from any item in the permanent collection of the library or archive in order to preserve or replace that item in the permanent collection of that library or archive or in the permanent collection of another prescribed library or archive.

(2) The prescribed conditions are:

(a) that the item in question is an item in the part of the permanent collection maintained by the library or archive wholly or mainly for the purposes of reference on the premises of the library or archive, or is an item in the permanent collection of the library or archive which is available on loan only to other libraries or archives;

(b) that it is not reasonably practicable for the librarian or archivist to purchase a copy of that item to fulfil the purpose under section 42(1)(a) or (b) of the Act;

(c) that the other prescribed library or archive furnishes a written statement to the effect that the item has been lost, destroyed or damaged and that it is not reasonably practicable for it to purchase a copy of that item, and that if a copy is supplied it will only be used to fulfil the purpose under section 42(1)(b) of the Act; and

(d) that the other prescribed library or archive shall be required to pay for the copy a sum not less than the cost (including a contribution to the general expenses of the library or archive) attributable to its production.

Copying by librarian or archivist of certain unpublished works

7. (1) For the purposes of section 43 of the Act the conditions specified in paragraph (2) of this regulation are prescribed as the conditions which must be complied with in the circumstances in which that section applies when the librarian or, as the case may be, the archivist makes and supplies a copy of the whole or part of a literary, dramatic or musical work from a document in the library or archive to a person requiring the copy.

(2) The prescribed conditions are:

(a) that no copy of the whole or part of the work shall be supplied to the person requiring the same unless

(i) he satisfies the librarian or archivist that he requires the copy for purposes of research or private study and will not use it for any other purpose; and

(ii) he has delivered to the librarian or, as the case may be, the archivist a declaration in writing, in relation to that work, substantially in accordance with Form B in Schedule 2 to these Regulations and signed in the manner therein indicated;

(b) that such person is not furnished with more than one copy of the same material; and

(c) that such person is required to pay for the copy a sum not less than the cost (including a contribution to the general expenses of the library or archive) attributable to its production.

(3)   Unless the librarian or archivist is aware that the signed declaration delivered to him pursuant to paragraph (2)(a)(ii) above is false in a material particular, he may rely on it as to the matter he is required to be satisfied on under paragraph (2)(a)(i) above before making or supplying the copy.

SCHEDULE I   Regulation 3

PART A   Regulation 3(1) and (3)

1. Any library administered by:
    (a) a library authority within the meaning of the Public Libraries and Museums Act 1964 in relation to England and Wales;
    (b) a statutory library authority within the meaning of the Public Libraries (Scotland) Act 1955, in relation to Scotland;
    (c) an Education and Library Board within the meaning of the Education and Libraries (Northern Ireland) Order 1986, in relation to Northern Ireland.

2. The British Library, the National Library of Wales, the National Library of Scotland, the Bodleian Library. Oxford and the University Library, Cambridge.

3. Any library of a school within the meaning of section 174 of the Act and any library of a description of educational establishment specified under that section in the Copyright (Educational Establishments) (No.2) Order 1989(d).

4. Any parliamentary library or library administered as part of a government department, including a Northern Ireland department, or any library conducted for or administered by an agency which is administered by a Minister of the Crown.

5. Any library administered by:
    (a) in England and Wales, a local authority within the meaning of the Local Government Act 1972, the Common Council of the City of London or the Council of the Isles of Scilly;
    (b) in Scotland, a local authority within the meaning of the Local Government (Scotland) Act 1973;
    (c) in Northern Ireland, a district council established under the Local Government Act (Northern Ireland) 1972.

6. Any other library conducted for the purpose of facilitating or encouraging the study of bibliography, education, fine arts, history, languages, law, literature, medicine, music, philosophy, religion, sci-

ence (including natural and social science) or technology, or administered by any establishment or organisation which is conducted wholly or mainly for such a purpose.

PART B   Regulation 3(3)

Any library outside the United Kingdom which is conducted wholly or mainly for the purpose of facilitating or encouraging the study of bibliography, education, fine arts, history, languages, law, literature, medicine. music, philosophy, religion. science (including natural and social science) or technology.

SCHEDULE 2

FORM A

DECLARATION: COPY OF ARTICLE OR PART OF PUBLISHED WORK

To:

The Librarian of _____ Library

[Address of Library]

Please supply me with a copy of:

*the article in the periodical, the particulars of which are

[   ]

*the part of the published work, the particulars of which are

[   ]

required by me for the purposes of research or private study.

2.   I declare that:

(a)   I have not previously been supplied with a copy of the same material by you or any other librarian;

(b)   I will not use the copy except for research or private study and will not supply a copy of it to any other person; and

(c)   to the best of my knowledge no other person with whom I work or study has made or intends to make, at or about the same time as this request, a request for substantially the same material for substantially the same purpose.

3.   I understand that if the declaration is false in a material particular the copy supplied to me by you will be an infringing copy and that I shall be liable for infringement of copyright as if I had made the copy myself.

†Signature _____

Date _____

Name   _____

Address   _____

               _____

               _____

*Delete whichever is inappropriate.

†This must be the personal signature of the person making the request. A stamped or typewritten signature, or the signature of an agent, is NOT acceptable.

FORM B

DECLARATION: COPY OF WHOLE OR PART OF UNPUBLISHED WORK

To

The *Librarian/Archivist of _____*Library/Archive

[Address of Library/Archive]

Please supply me with a copy of:

the *whole/following part [particulars of part] of the [particulars of the unpublished work] required by me for the purposes of research or private study.

2.   I declare that:

  (a)   I have not previously been supplied with a copy of the same material by you or any other librarian or archivist;

  (b)   I will not use the copy except for research or private study and will not supply a copy of it to any other person; and

  (c)   to the best of my knowledge the work had not been published before the document was deposited in your *library/archive and the copyright owner has not prohibited copying of the work.

3.   I understand that if the declaration is false in a material particular the copy supplied to me by you will be an infringing copy and that I shall be liable for infringement of copyright as if I had made the copy myself.

†Signature _____

Date _____

Name   _____

Address   _____

　　　　　　 _____

　　　　　　 _____

*Delete whichever is inappropriate.

†This must be the personal signature of the person making the request. A stamped or typewritten signature, or the signature of an agent, is NOT acceptable.

SI 96/2967 The Copyright and Related Rights Regulations 1996

PART II

AMENDMENTS OF THE COPYRIGHT, DESIGNS AND PATENTS ACT 1988

Rental or lending of copyright work

10. (1) In section 16 (the acts restricted by copyright in a work), in subsection (1), after paragraph (b) insert '(ba) to rent or lend the work to the public (see section 18A);'

(2) After section 18 (infringement of copyright by issue of copies of work), insert

18A. (1) The rental or lending of copies of the work to the public is an act restricted by the copyright in

(a) a literary, dramatic or musical work,

(b) an artistic work, other than

  (i) a work of architecture in the form of a building or a model for a building, or

  (ii) a work of applied art, or

(c) a film or a sound recording.

(2) In this Part, subject to the following provisions of this section

(a) "rental" means making a copy of the work available for use, on terms that it will or may be returned, for direct or indirect economic or commercial advantage, and

(b) "lending" means making a copy of the work available for use, on terms that it will or may be returned, otherwise than for direct or indirect economic or commercial advantage, through an establishment which is accessible to the public

(3) The expressions "rental" and "lending" do not include

(a)　making available for the purpose of public performance, playing or showing in public, broadcasting or inclusion in a cable programme service;

(b)　making available for the purpose of exhibition in public; or

(c)　making available for on-the-spot reference use.

(4)　The expression "lending" does not include making available between establishments which are accessible to the Dublin

(5)　Where lending by an establishment accessible to the public gives rise to a payment the amount of which does not go beyond what is necessary to cover the operating costs of the establishment, there is no direct or indirect economic or commercial advantage for the purposes of this section.

(6)　References in this Part to the rental or lending of copies of a work include the rental or lending of the original."

(3)　"rental right" means the right of a copyright owner to authorise or prohibit the rental of copies of the work

Permitted lending of copyright works

11.　(1)　In Chapter III of Part I (acts permitted in relation to copyright works), in the sections relating to education, after section 36 insert

'36A. Copyright in a work is not infringed by the lending of copies of the by an educational establishment'.

(2)　In the same Chapter, in the sections relating to libraries and archives, after section 40 insert

'40A. (1) Copyright in a work of any description is not infringed by the lending of a book by a public library if the book is within the public lending right scheme.

For this purpose:

(a)　"the public lending right scheme" means the scheme in force under section I of the Public Lending Right Act 1979, and

(b)　a book is within the public lending right scheme if it is a book within the meaning of the provisions of the scheme relating to eligibility, whether or not it is in fact eligible.

(2) Copyright in a work is not infringed by the lending of copies of the work by a prescribed library or archive (other than a public library) which is not conducted for profit"

(3) In the same Chapter for section 66 (rental of sound recordings, films and computer programs), and the heading preceding it. substitute

Publication right

16. (1) A person who after the expiry of copyright protection, publishes for the first time a previously unpublished work has, in accordance with the following provisions, a property right ("publication right") equivalent to copyright.

(2) For this purpose publication includes any communication to the public, in particular

(a) the issue of copies to the public;

(b) making the work available by means of an electronic retrieval system;

(c) the rental or lending of copies of the work to the public;

(d) the performance, exhibition or showing of the work in public; or

(e) broadcasting the work or including it in a cable programme service.

(3) No account shall be taken for this purpose of any unauthorised act.

In relation to a time when there is no copyright in the work, an unauthorised act means an act done without the consent of the owner of the physical medium in which the work is embodied or on which it is recorded.

(4) A work qualifies for publication right protection only if

(a) first publication is in the European Economic Area, and

(b) the publisher of the work is at the time of first publication a national of an EEA state.

(6)   Publication right expires at the end of the period of 25 years from the end of the calendar year in which the work was first published.

(7)   In this regulation a "work" means a literary, dramatic, musical or artistic work or a film.'

Lending of copies by educational establishments

6A. (1)   The rights conferred by Part II are not infringed by the lending of copies of a recording of a performance by an educational establishment.

Lending of copies by libraries or archives

6B. (1)   The rights conferred by Part II are not infringed by the lending of copies of a recording of a performance by a prescribed library or archive (other than a public library) which is not conducted for profit.

Lending of certain recordings

14A. (1)   The Secretary of State may by order provide that in such cases as may be specified in the order the lending to the public of copies of films or sound recordings shall be treated as licensed by the performer subject only to the payment of such reasonable royalty or other payment as may be agreed or determined in default of agreement by the Copyright Tribunal.

Index

Please note that index references are to the numbered paragraphs, not to pages.